Feng shui

for modern living

Feng Shui

for modern living

Stephen Skinner

with

Mary Lambert

風水 FENG SHUI
FOR MODERN LIVING

T
Trafalgar Square Publishing

First published in the United States of America in 2000 by
Trafalgar Square Publishing, North Pomfret, Vermont 05053

Reproduction by Alliance Graphics, Singapore
Printed and bound in Portugal by Printer Portuguesa

ISBN 1-57076-161-2

Library of Congress Catalog Card Number: 99-69289

10 9 8 7 6 5 4 3 2

Project Editor: Mary Lambert

Designed by Sara Kidd

Cover designed by Roger Daniels

contents

introduction

Feng shui, which literally means 'wind' and 'water' is the ancient art of furniture placement and energy flow in the home which has been practised successfully in China for several thousand years.

In the West it is now much more widely accepted as a practice – people who have embraced all the principles have found how it has improved the atmosphere in their homes, their relationships with their family, and, in turn, affected their wellbeing, giving them new energy to change and improve their lives.

How does it work?

Feng shui works on the basis that energy currents, known as *ch'i*, flow through the home. In Japan this energy is known as *ki* and in India it is called *Prana*. So, to get the best from our living area, these currents need tobe able to flow freely throughout the home and not become blocked or stagnant.

The first part of this book, *Energize your life with feng shui* discusses the different aspects of feng shui and talks about how *ch'i* also flows through our surrounding environment and our bodies. Therapies such as Chinese herbalism, acupuncture and shiatsu use a detailed system of diagnosis to find energy blockages in the body. They then prescribe treatments, tailored to the individual, to sutbtly manipulate the energy flow so that any blockages causing illness or discomfort are corrected or removed.

Ch'i always moves in spirals and this movement needs to be encouraged in the home. Sharp angles on furniture, deep corners or beams can distort this flow causing straight poison arrows, or cutting, *sha ch'i* to be directed at the occupants.

►

A home always needs to have a good mixture of *yin* and *yang* qualities to create harmony and balance. Soft textures and tactile fabrics are very *yin*.

Long-term exposure to this bad energy can bring about upset or illness. Cures, such as hanging crystals or plants, can be used to break up or screen this type of energy.

Yin and yang

A central part of feng shui is the balance of the opposing forces of *yin* and *yang*. *Yin* is seen as female, dark and passive, while the *yang* qualities are male, positive, bright and fiery. The *tai ch'i* symbol shows the interaction of *yin* and *yang* – one cannot operate without the other. *Yin* is the earth, darkness, the moon and death, while *yang* is heaven, light, the sun and life. Each depends on the other to exist.

In the context of the home there always needs to be a balance of *yin* and *yang* energies for perfect harmony. For example, in a living room you need to mix accessories such as a hardwood table, a mirror and metal ornaments – which are all *yang* – with cushions, a throw, a rug and curtains – which are all *yin*. Having too many objects of one force in a setting immediately creates an imbalance in a room's energies.

The compass

Before you can start working on improvements in your home you need to find out the direction of your house using a basic orienteering compass. This enables you to discover where the Elements – the core energies present everywhere which shape and transform all life – lie and where the eight aspirations are located. These are the areas that you can then enhance in your home.

◄ Lavender essential oil, made from the lavender flowers, is very healing. It is good for space clearing where, mixed with water, it clears negative energies.

▼ Aromatic soaps and bath salts and lotions can make the bathroom a very pleasant environment.

The Five Elements

The Five Elements are associated with the eight compass directions: the South is Fire, the North is Water, the East is Wood and the West is Metal. The Southwest is Strong Earth, the Northwest is Strong Metal, the Northeast is Small Earth and the Southeast is Small Wood.

The relationship between these Five Elements, the compass directions and the *pa kua* are the core of feng shui practice. By knowing how each Element relates to the other, the feng shui practitioner can interpret how the Five Elements work together in the world to create good and bad luck, and start to influence them.

The Elements are controlled by two cycles – the Productive Cycle and the Destructive Cycle. In the Productive Cycle, for example, Fire produces Earth which in turn produces Metal and so forth.

The Destructive Cycle reflects the decaying process that is ongoing in nature. So in this cycle Wood breaks up Earth, which then absorbs Water and so on. The understanding of these two cycles helps feng shui practitioners to use symbolic items relating to these Elements to enhance a sector of the *pa kua*, and ensure others are not used in sectors where they would clash with the dominant, ruling Element.

The *pa kua*

The *pa kua* is an eight-sided octagon figure with a trigram on each side that is one of the basic diagnostic tools used in feng shui. To map out your home, take the compass direction with an orienteering compass. Once a plan of your home has been drawn with the compass direction in position, the *pa kua* can be put on top with the eight trigrams showing the eight directions.

The Eight Aspirations

Each sector of the *pa kua* represents one of the Eight Aspirations: South is Recognition and Fame, North is Career Prospects, East is Family and Health, West is Children, Southwest is Marriage and Romantic Happiness, Northwest is Mentors and Networking, Northeast is Education and Knowledge and Southeast is Wealth and Prosperity.

When the *pa kua* is placed on your home's plan you can see in which areas the Aspirations are located. You can then utilize the relevant Elements to begin enhancing them according to the your best directions.

Planning your home

Once you understand the basics of feng shui and have superimposed your *pa kua* on the plan of your home you can start to have fun.

Every room in the home, as well as the garden, is discussed in detail, with useful information on what areas might need attention to enhance your personal aspirations with all part of your interior decoration, from textures, lighting, furniture to furnishings.

For example, it is important to have a high proportion of *yang* textures in a bathroom to counteract the *yin* aspect of this water-draining room. In a bedroom, lighting is important to bring in *yang* energy, but it must not be harsh which will upset the tranquil environment.

Using feng shui techniques can be immensely rewarding. But do not try to do too much at once. Start with one room and see the amazing effect it can have on you and your family – then work through the rest of your home and your life.

► Before you can start to apply any feng shui enhancements in your home, you need to clear out any unwanted or broken items as these only create stagnant energies. Keep the things that you are attached to but plan your storage carefully and remember it need not be conventional in style, these straw baskets look very eyecatching on this unit.

◄ Stone pots are aesthetically very pleasing. As they are linked to the Earth Element they can be placed in the living room or the garden to enhance the Southwest or Northeast sectors.

ENER

your
life
with
feng
shui

GIZE

Feng shui is an ancient discipline that affects not only your home and environment, but also your life. Once you begin to make changes within your home your energy levels will change, as will your outlook on life. But, before placing enhancements in your Aspiration corners, clear out any clutter and negative energies which may be holding you back, not forgetting to look at your body energies within. Therapies, such as acupuncture and shiatsu, can remove internal blockages and restore inner peace.

Feng shui
for balanced living

While the disciplines of acupuncture and Chinese martial arts are already well established and respected in the West, feng shui, which deals with the art of placement and energy flow in the home, is now quickly catching up and gaining mainstream acceptance.

The thing that distinguishes all these Chinese arts from western arts is that their theoretical basis derives from a totally different view of the universe. Western "science" does not find feng shui easy to accept, even when it works time and time again, when its theoretical roots do not fit with the much more limited western view of the universe.

The solution is to stand back and see what feng shui can do for you in your home. Only when you see what the results are, can you decide for yourself whether you would like to get involved more in the theory. Once you appreciate how it works, it all begins to make sense, and then feng shui can be used not only to make simple decorative changes in your home but also to improve the overall quality of your life—in all areas. The location of your house, how its furniture and contents are arranged, how color is used in each room, and how the *ch'i* flows all contribute to a balanced or unbalanced, a positive or negative enviornment. By using feng shui techniques these basic elements

can be manipulated to create a harmonious, balanced area that gives you happiness, wealth, and good health.

The origins of feng shui
Feng shui (pronounced foong-schway) means wind and water. Basically all life on this planet, from the rocks in the mountains underfoot to the weather and moods of the heavens, is affected

by wind and water, and is animated by what is known as the life force, or energy—*ch'i* (pronounced chee). *Ch'i* flows through everything: wherever *ch'i* is concentrated you will find that plants, animals, and people flourish and multiply. *Ch'i* is most often found concentrated where water flows slowly and sinuously. Why, for example, are most of the great cities of the world built on sheltered harbors or slow-

◄

Slow moving "shui" or water is considered to be where the most *ch'i* or energy gathers, which is why it is thought that many successful cities are built on rivers.

◄
The elaborate *lo pa'an* compass is used by Chinese feng shui consultants to map out a home, but an ordinary compass will give you all the directional information that you need.

►
***Ch'i* is also inside our bodies and if we have blockages or imbalances our health suffers and we can become ill. Complementary therapies such as acupuncture or Chinese herbalism can help to harmonize our body energies.**

flowing rivers? These sites accumulate *ch'i* which subsequently encourages life and help to stimulate trade.

Where *ch'i* stagnates and forms backwaters, life eventually loses its resilience, decays and dies. Where *ch'i* rushes past, such as at river rapids, no beneficial life force can accumulate and there are few people who can live here either. *Ch'i* works on many different levels and affects everything around us.

The psychology of feng shui

A beneficial concentration of *ch'i* does not just favor plants and animals, it also helps give us our positive attitude to life, our hopes and dreams, and the energy that we have to make them come real.

Concentrations of *ch'i* also affect our emotions and attitude to life. We all know how depression (associated with stagnant *ch'i*) robs us of the power

to plan ahead, to move forward, to grow, with the result that one setback follows on the heels of another, as if life was conspiring against us. But when we are feeling strong, when *ch'i* is present in abundance, no challenge is too great for us. If we fail, we just pick ourselves up and try again.

A positive attitude by itself is sometimes hard to maintain in the face of adversity, but the right concentrations of beneficial *ch'i* make this so much easier. A rather watered down western version of this effect is how we all recognize that our surroundings can make us feel uplifted or depressed. You intuitively know when your environment feels uncomfortable but can't quite put a finger on why. The feng shui practitioner looks beyond the superficial layout of a home or office and checks out the subtle configuration of *ch'i*, sensing where there are

blockages or stagnation which can really affect and determine our moods.

Fate and luck

The roots of Western civilization in Europe, Australia, and North America are buried in Classical Greece, where the prevailing view of life was to consider ourselves the "playthings of fate." "Luck" is something that in the West is seen as capricious as the numbers in a lottery. Luck, for the Chinese, however, was something that could be encouraged and cultivated, something at least partly within our own control. How else, they reasoned, could some people be consistently lucky and others not so, if luck was really governed only by the so called "laws of chance."

The ancient Chinese thought that there were three types of luck. First the luck you are born with (this explains the inequality of opportunity according to the family you were born into) and this is called "Heaven Luck."

The second category, called "Man Luck," is the luck we make ourselves; the efforts of a "self-made man" fall into this category. Lastly, but not least, is "Earth Luck," and this is the luck we can engineer by skillfully applying the principles of feng shui. Feng shui practices can affect different concentrations of *ch'i* and so specific types of luck associated with life's various aspirations such as health, wealth, and family happiness. This type of luck can never be fully understood until you have actually either applied feng shui yourself, or had a professional practitioner make the correct changes for you.

Health

Ch'i affects much more than just our emotions, it also affects our physical strength, even our resistance to disease. Just as *ch'i* helps the martial arts master to perform apparently superhuman feats of strength, so a beneficial concentration of *ch'i* can help encourage the body's natural healing process.

Relationships and career

Implementing good feng shui changes in the home can strengthen our mental outlook and increase our energy levels. It can also improve the way we interact with other people, making other people's perceptions of us stronger and much more positive. This in turn strengthens our existing family relationships, or attracts new people into our social environment. Relationships within the family with your

◄ By making feng shui changes to your home and boosting the relevant area, you can strengthen and improve your relationship with your partner.

► By increasing the energy in the home and bringing in more beneficial *ch'i*, your career will benefit and more prosperity will come into your life.

own children will also be affected if specific feng shui formulas are activated by you.

Wealth

When you get promoted in your career, it obviously improves your financial position, but feng shui goes further than this and proposes that

accumulations of subtle and beneficial *ch'i* will work themselves through to the physical plane in terms of increased business opportunities and the real accumulation of corresponding wealth.

Feng shui practice

The practice of feng shui is not "hocus pocus" but is a very well thought out,

◄
When the *ch'i* flows well in your home environment, you will find that you interact better with friends and attract new ones.

practice, but there are several less obvious ones which come with more advanced practice, not least of all is an increase in spiritual clarity, and an ability to see some of the underlying causes of change in both your own and other people's lives, and the material world. You no longer need to leave events to fate, because with your new knowledge you can choose to "go with the flow" and consciously move at the correct time in the direction you wish to go in.

You would be right if you felt this sounded like a simplification of Taoist philosophy, for feng shui is, in fact, one of the early Taoist practices. But do remember that feng shui is not a religious belief, it is a technique, sometimes a science, and often an art that works to create balance, order and harmony in your home, environment and your life.

specific method—different formulas are used to promote health, relationships or to prevent quarrelling within the family. You can quite easily gain enough information to improve your own feng shui environment, but take care how you implement it as a little knowledge can definitely be a dangerous thing. Make no mistake, a change of your feng shui for the worse will soon reflect itself in your life, just as a beneficial change will do just the reverse. Feng shui is a disciplined technique—there is no question of faith. It works with or without faith. So it can be better to call in a feng shui expert if you do not have the time to learn the subject yourself, but need some rapid results.

These are just some of the more obvious benefits of correct feng shui

chinese language

Although it is not necessary to recognize key Chinese characters to appreciate the principles of feng shui, they are included in this book where they might be useful. All Chinese characters will be transliterated using the Wade-Giles system of rendering Chinese, rather than the modern *pinyin* system used in mainland China. This is simply because, until recently, over 95 per cent of all feng shui books printed in English used this system. To have used the *pinyin* system would have meant alienating many people who have already got used to seeing feng shui explained in the more familiar forms of the Wades-Giles system. For Chinese readers this does not present a problem, where the original Chinese character is present.

The influence of
yin and yang

▲
The *tai ch'i yin* and *yang* symbol shows how the dark *yin* (passive) and the white *yang* (positive) energy are **together in a united circle. It highlights the fact that nothing is ever totally *yin* or totally *yang*, but a mixture of both.**

Yin and *yang* are interactive terms that are used to compare everything that exists or lives in the world. They are often described as complementary but opposite states.

Yin has traditionally been associated with the Earth and the female in our environment. Its qualities include the winter, the cold, the dark, stillness, negativity and water. *Yang*, on the other hand, represents Heaven, the male, infinity or the cosmos. *Yang's* nature is warm, well lit, bright, fiery, positive, dry, moving, and living.

Yin and *yang* symbol
The Taoist *tai ch'i* symbol simplifies the relationship of *yin* with *yang*. The circle shows unity, while the shaded section represents the darker *yin* energy with the white section representing the lighter, brighter *yang* energy. Within each section there is a small pinpoint of its opposite energy. This emphasizes the principle that nothing is totally *yin* and nothing is totally *yang* – there has to be a small amount of the opposite present to give it some dynamism.

The earliest interpretation of *yin* and *yang* in feng shui is in the Form School which deals with the environment. Here *yin* represents the cold, darker, shady, North-facing side of a hill whereas *yang* represents the warmer, brighter, well-lit, sunnier, South-facing slope. Also the landscape is viewed as mountains or water. Mountains are still and *yin*, while water is *yang* and active. So the ideal site has both hills and rivers.

The modern interpretation
In feng shui, *yin* and *yang* can provide us with a starting point when we look at our home or office. Homes should be three parts *yang* to two parts *yin*. The difference between these two environments is that a home is where we restore our energy and need to feel protected. So the home should be more *yin* than the office space which needs to be *yang*, active, bright, and highly charged for positive work.

◄
Soft, luxurious throws will bring in more *yin* qualities to your living room.

▲
A *yang* glass dish
can be used to
offset the *yin*
qualities of soft
furnishings.

◄
Metal ornaments
are strong, positive
items to place in a
corner of a living
or dining room.

▲
**You can
manipulate and
balance the energy
in a room by
adding *yin* and
yang elements.
This hardwood
table brings in
more *yang*.**

Your home could be rural (more *yin*) or
urban (relatively more *yang*). Is it an
old, period property (more *yin*) or a
modern house (*yang*)?

In furnishings, for example, gilded
paintings, stone sculptures, metal
furniture, and mirrors are very *yang*,
while upholstered furniture, fabric
wallhangings or large cushions are
more *yin*. With colours, red and
orange, for example, are good to
boost your Southwest relationship
corners and introduce more *yang*,
while blue, black, and green bring in
more *yin* qualities.

Harmonizing the two qualities of
yin and *yang* in all your rooms will
help to bring about contentment and
balance in your home, creating
happiness in your life.

YIN AND YANG FOR THE HOME tips

❍ Enhance *yin* with a relaxing and warm
décor, soft furnishings, and relaxing music.
❍ The bedroom needs to be calm, because
this is where we restore energy through sleep.
Yang electrical items such as TVs, stereos, and
work-related fax machines or computers
should be avoided.
❍ Candles in the living areas will bring in
some positive *yang* energy.
❍ Kitchens need to be more *yang* because
this is where the family regularly gathers to eat
meals and to be nourished. Bright lighting,
electrical appliances, fridges, freezers, hobs
and ovens or cookers all enhance the
presence of this strong energy.
❍ Encourage *yang* energy to enter and flow
well through your home by keeping your
hallway uncluttered.

clearing the
clutter

▲
In the bathroom or on a dressing table, small sisal baskets can hold make-up and other toiletries which can otherwise look messy on shelves.

►
Boxes, in stylish white, can provide vital storage in a home office creating a neat, tidy environment.

◄
A free-standing wardrobe provides a practical and refreshing change from heavy, fitted versions. Put away any clothes that you have worn before you go to sleep, so that you are not surrounded by unsettling mess.

In feng shui terms, if you want to create a new future for yourself, then first you need to clear out any clutter so that you can make some space for new possibilities and opportunities to enter into your life.

It seems the more items that we have in our homes, the more they begin to drag us down. So why do we get so attached to everything? Why are we so reluctant to throw out articles that we don't use any more?

Deciding whether to keep or throw out our precious belongings can be a difficult choice. But before you throw everything away and become a minimalist, it is essential to differentiate between storing things you want to keep and what you would call clutter. Things that you want to keep should be useful, be stored tidily, and be easily accessible. Clutter on the other hand, is anything that you no longer wear or which is no longer being used and does not have a proper home.

Don't hang onto things such as old clothes thinking that you might wear them one day or need them for a fancy dress party. Clutter can have a significant effect on us by impeding the smooth flow of *ch'i* around the home, reducing the chances of us progressing through life with ease and comfort. If you surround yourself with things that you want and love, your energy will increase every time you see them.

Planning good storage

A well-designed storage system should be tailored to the individual and be something that you can control, rather than the other way around. If you want to create a new future for yourself, then clear the clutter and make some space in your life for new possibilities and opportunities to enter.

Look around your home and see where your clutter is. Then work out how it relates to the *pa kua* and your Best Directions. For example, if there is a mountain of old newspapers destined for recycling in your Career corner than you could expect this to symbolize, and even cause, a lack of progress in your chosen career.

◄
Colorful, stacking boxes take up little space, and can be used in bedrooms or home offices to tidy away a variety of items.

CLEARING THE CLUTTER tips

Clutter creates obstruction in your life. By having a major clear-out you will notice how your life starts to move on.

❍ Keep the hallway and stairs free of boxes, newspaper, or toys to let *ch'i* flow in freely.

❍ Throw out old items you don't need or use, you will feel so much better.

❍ Give good clothes that you no longer wear to a charity shop and keep a "capsule" wardrobe.

❍ Mend any broken appliances or throw them out and feel how your energy increases.

❍ Always remove clutter before using any feng shui enhancements.

❍ Clear paperwork from your home desk regularly, prioritize tasks and urgent calls, so that you keep on top.

❍ Don't keep rubbish under the bed or old electrical equipment as this creates negative, stagnant energy.

You need to plan storage for your entire home, and not do it on a piecemeal basis. When you think about where you could add storage facilities, bear in mind that locating storage in your most inauspicious Directions is a good way of making sure that the bad *ch'i* stays trapped and out of harm's way. Never put storage in your auspicious Directions because it is stagnant energy and will create the same effect in areas that should be activated, i.e. your *sheng ch'i* (or Best Direction).

Now work out your storage requirements, but remember to think about any possible problems, such as blocking off electric sockets, hinged doors, the height of the storage systems and not being able to reach them, and the strength of your walls for shelving. Your ultimate goal should be to surround yourself with vibrant and free-flowing *ch'i* energy. You should also be able to find things that you need more

easily, you'll create more space to do what you like, you will also probably reveal hidden architectural features or parts of furniture when you have removed unwanted clutter.

Stylish storage

You can still be imaginative when tackling your storage needs. By breaking away from conventional storage solutions and improvising with colorful boxes or crates, for example, it is possible not only to find a sense of individual style that suits your tastes, but also to produce storage results that work really well.

You may even find the answer to your storage problems by looking at what was used in another period in history—English country classics or cool 20th-century contemporary interiors, for example. Alternatively, you may find your solution by looking back at the thousands of years of rich, colorful ethnic style.

▲
Colorful, stacking baskets made of wicker can serve a dual purpose in a living room: they can store away magazines, newspapers, and other paraphernalia and be chosen to blend in with the room's decor.

◄
Little baskets are so versatile and can be displayed in any room in your home. In the kitchen they can be filled up with seasonal fruit.

►
If you want to incorporate large stacking units in a room, try and place them in a corner which otherwise would be rather negative or unused space.

◀

By carefully planning your storage units you can house all your treasured possessions. Be careful of having too many open shelves, however, as their sharp edges can send out cutting *ch'i* into the room.

◀

Storage items can be inventive. These battered old suitcases add a faded charm to this room, as well as usefully housing possessions.

CLEARING THE CLUTTER

checklist

❍ Think about the kind of storage that you want—does it need to be flexible or permanent?

❍ Calculate how much you can spend on storage units.

❍ Look to see if there is any extra space in your home you could use for storage only.

❍ Decide which objects need to be stored away, and where. Work out if they need to be put away in certain rooms, e.g. sports equipment/hobbies.

❍ Think where to put important items that you always have problems finding, e.g. passport.

❍ Plan storage for sentimental items that you don't look at often, such as love letters or holiday mementoes.

❍ Organize where to put seasonal items, e.g. winter or summer clothes.

Space
clearing

One fascinating adjunct to feng shui is Space Clearing. This ancient art clears any inauspicious energy in the home and office through the use of ceremony and ritual. This practice is traditionally used before moving into a new home or after there has been an illness or a misfortune. It may also be used to maximize the effectiveness of feng shui "cures" and can help to clear any stagnant areas in a room.

The difference between a room before and after a Space Clearing is tangible—rooms that have been cleared feel lighter and brighter, like a fresh spring breeze has flung open the windows. After a house has had a Space Clearing it can feel like you are walking through a forest with tall, stately evergreen trees. The air can seem so fresh. The lingering smell of pine needles can clear your head. A home can feel very good and give all the occupants a feeling of exhilaration.

Feng shui and Space Clearing

Space Clearing, which is used in conjunction with Chinese feng shui can be found in similar forms in diverse cultures throughout the world. For example in China, to clear a home of negative *ch'i* energy a Taoist priest writes prayers on parchment paper. He then burns the prayers and mixes the ashes with salt and ceremoniously sprinkles the salt mixture throughout the home. Similar rituals using salt for Space Clearing have been used in almost every culture around the world. Although many of the Space Clearing traditions that have evolved over time are complex and involved, there are some simple methods that anyone can use to shift the atmosphere of a room and raise its energy level.

Moving into a new home or business

It is essential to purify the energies of a home or business before moving in, otherwise the residual energies of the

◄
A few drops of essential oils mixed with water in a mister can be used to Space Clear a room. Geranium or lavender are very good to use after an argument.

►
When a room has been Space Cleared you will immediately notice the change in the atmosphere. It will seem very light and airy like a fresh spring day.

previous residents will continue to be felt by the new occupants. Often the history of a home or business can be very revealing. For example, in one case, three residents living successively in the same home, at different times, were each in severe car accidents. In another case, two separate occupants of the same home developed the exact same rare kind of leukaemia. After moving into the same home, three separate homeowners became alcoholics. Coincidence? A feng shui practitioner would say that residual energies that are not cleared continue to subconsciously affect future residents.

Although a Space Clearing by a professional consultant is recommended before a move, there are some things that anyone can do beforehand. If possible, do a complete cleansing of walls, ceilings, and floors. One tradition advocates placing nine orange, lemon, or lime skins in a bowl, then filling the bowl with water and splashing the water on all surfaces. Another method is to burn a small amount of sage in each room while holding the thought or intention that the energy in the room is being purified.

Clearing stagnant energy

Stagnant energy affects the health and wellbeing of the occupants of the home and Space Clearing techniques can help bring in vital new life force into a building. Energy becomes especially lifeless in the corners of a room because energy (*ch'i*) travels in circular, spiral movements which pass by corners. This movement can be compared to water flowing down a mountain stream. Where there is an inside bend in a stream, silt, leaves,

sticks, and debris collect. Corners of rooms are similar as they tend to be the places in the room where energy goes dormant or stagnant. Space Clearing can bring a vitality back to those areas. However, after a while, the energy can become sluggish again in those corners and may need to be cleared once more.

Clearing negativity

If you have ever walked into a room after there has been an argument you know that heavy, dense feeling that resides in the room long after the argument is finished. This is an example of negative *ch'i* and it can

affect the health and wellbeing of anyone who enters the room until it is cleared. In addition, if someone has been ill in a house for a while or if at any time life hasn't been flowing well or if your business reaches a standstill, there may be negative *ch'i* in the room or building that needs Space Clearing.

Clearing out clutter

A good first step for Space Clearing is to clear out any clutter (see pages 18–21). Clutter affects the flow of *ch'i* and slows its energy and movement. Removing clutter can help to free restricted energy and it can symbolically remove things that have

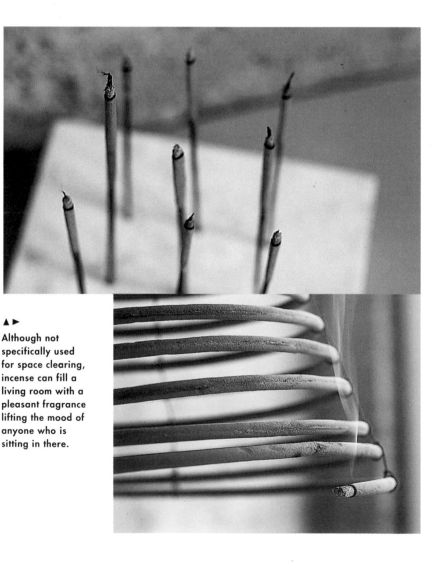

▲ ▶
Although not specifically used for space clearing, incense can fill a living room with a pleasant fragrance lifting the mood of anyone who is sitting in there.

▲
Stagnant energy can often gather in the corners of living areas. It may need to be cleared, using the methods described in the Tips box, on a regular basis.

been weighing you down. After clearing the clutter, stand in the middle of the room to be cleared. Take a very deep breath and expand your awareness to fill all of the room. Then circle the room using a bell, rattle, or drum to make a sound. Allow your intention to follow the sound and to fill the room. Keep going round the room in circles until you start to feel that the room is lighter and clearer.

Before placing feng shui cures

Space Clearing is excellent to do before installing any feng shui cures, because putting a cure in before a space is cleared can be likened to picking a beautiful bouquet of flowers but putting them in a vase still filled with the old dried flowers.

Whether you are hanging a lead crystal or installing a fish tank, the results will last longer and be more potent if the space has been cleared of any negative energy first.

SIMPLE SPACE CLEARING tips

Space Clearing is needed after moving into a new home or office, after there has been an illness in the home, after an argument and generally when a room feels stagnant and before feng shui cures are implemented. By using these simple techniques you can create a fresh welcoming atmosphere in the rooms that have been cleared.

❍ Clap your hands briskly as you circle the room. Pay particular attention to corners and dark areas. Clap from floor to ceiling. The sound will become crisper as the energy in the room clears.

❍ Spray a room using a water mister (ideally glass) and a few drops of essential oil.

❍ With a new home use sage, pine, fir, or juniper oil.

❍ After an illness spray with eucalyptus, lemon, or rosemary.

❍ After an argument fill with lavender or geranium.

❍ To lift the energy use some orange, lemongrass, lime, or peppermint.

❍ Start in the easternmost corner and ring a bell as you start to circle the room. Hold the thought in your mind of the sound waves carrying your intention throughout every part of the area. Complete the Space Clearing by moving the bell in a figure of eight which completes the clearing and "ties the room off."

❍ Sprinkle salt crystals throughout the circumference of the room. Pay particular attention to the corners. The salt can be vacuumed up after 24 hours.

Feng shui basics
for the home

To map out your home and find where the eight Aspirations are you first need to find its compass directions. Although traditionally, the feng shui practitioner used a highly complex and expensive Chinese compass, or *lo p'an*, to map out properties, there is no need for you to race out and buy one. Any good quality standard orienteering compass will work just as well.

Using the *pa kua*

The *pa kua* (or *ba gua* if you prefer the pinyin version of the Chinese) is one of the basic diagnostic tools used in feng shui. it is a simple eight-sided figure, an octagon. *Pa* means "eight" while *kua* means "trigram," hence *pa kua* simply means eight trigrams.

When the *pa kua* is superimposed on the plan of a home it can be used for feng shui diagnosis. These *pa kua* directions are very versatile, they can be applied either to a whole house, its garden, an apartment, or just a single room. Used in this way the eight trigrams are allocated to each of the eight main compass directions. Traditional Chinese feng shui orientates the *Li* trigram to magnetic South.

The inner ring shows the trigrams and how they relate to the compass points, the second ring features the Chinese name of the trigram, for example, Sun is the name of the trigram in the Southeast, the third ring relates to the Chinese Elements. Wood,

Metal, and Earth have two directions, while Fire and Water have just one, the fourth ring shows the colour of each Element. The fifth ring shows the eight compass directions. Use these to place the *pa kua* symbol over a plan of your home and divide it into eight sectors. The sixth ring shows the aspect of life's typical aspirations—the Southwest, for example, corresponds with romantic or marital relationships (see also pages 46–47).

Using the *pa kua*

The eight sectors of the *pa kua* each represent one of the eight Aspirations (see pages 42–57), and each is attributed to a different facet of your life. By following these five easy steps, you can find out where your eight Aspirations are located in your home and apply feng shui techniques to increase your chances of health, wealth, and happiness:

1 Draw a floor plan to scale of the room you wish to focus on, or of the whole house or apartment.

2 Find the center of the area on the plan by drawing two diagonal lines and finding where they cross. Mark this point so the compass can be positioned here.

3 Mark the four compass points—North, East, South and West—and the four mid-points—Northeast, Southeast, Southwest and Northwest—on the plan.

4 Superimpose the *pa kua* symbol (as shown right) over the plan matching the compass points to the corresponding *pa kua* divisions.

5 Make a note of the areas of your home and their relevant Aspiration and location for quick reference (see box on page 28).

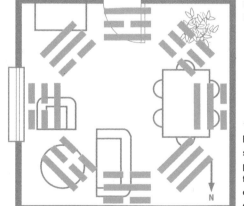

◄ Place the *pa kua* symbol over the plan of your home to find the location of the Aspirations and their trigrams.

▼
Photostat this *pa kua* image and place over your house, apartment or individual room plan making sure that you carefully match up the compass points.

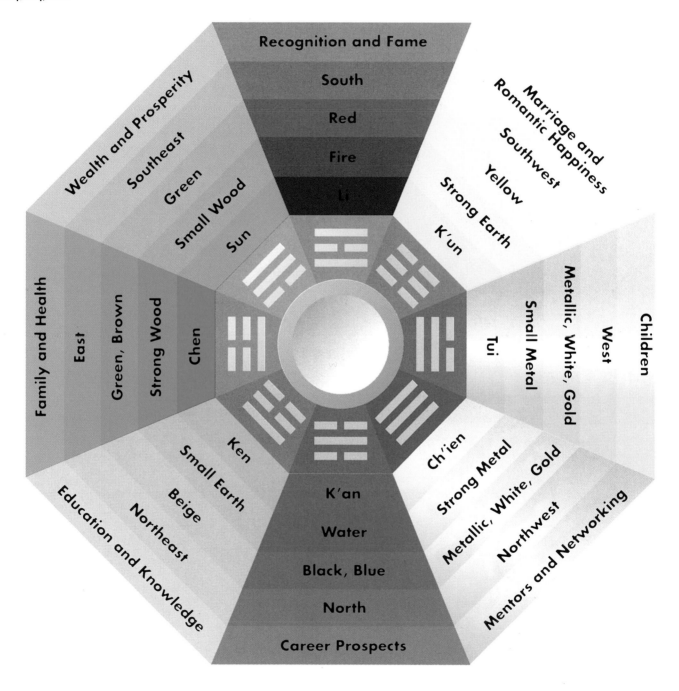

Missing corners

It is worth noting that this method works best when the shape of the house is either rectangle or square. If you have an irregular shaped house or apartment, perhaps an L-shaped or irregular shaped one, you will have a "missing corner." In feng shui terms this indicates that there will be one or more *pa kua* sectors missing, effectively preventing that area from being energized or enhanced. This can be compensated for by the careful placement of lights and mirrors to fill in the missing sector symbolically.

In essence, if you want a simple and efficient means of improving the feng shui of your home or garden, then look no further than the *pa kua*. When coupled with a compass, the two make DIY feng shui both easy and fun. All you have to do is decide on which type of Aspiration you want to stimulate and then get to work enhancing it.

The eight *pa kua* sectors

North	Career
Northeast	Education and Knowledge
East	Family and Health
Southeast	Wealth and Prosperity
South	Fame and Recognition
Southwest	Relationships and Marriage
West	Children
Northwest	Mentors and Networking

► Mapping out your living room can be fun because once you know its sectors you can choose furnishings and accessories to boost the relevant Aspiration.

► An irregular-shaped home will have one or more *pa kua* sectors missing. This means that this corner's luck cannot be easily energized. To find the missing sector, draw two diagonal lines on your plan to find the center point and position the compass here.

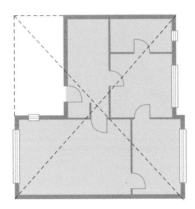

◄ Once you have mapped out your home with a compass and the *pa kua*, you may want to map out rooms, such as the bedroom, individually so that you can enhance its relevent sectors.

The five
elements

It has been said that by combining the five Elements in different quantities it is possible to create all the permutations found in nature. But when applied to feng shui, it becomes obvious that the five Elements have a particularly special relationship with the eight sectors of the *pa kua* (see pages 26–29).

The Productive and Destructive Cycles

The relationship between the five Elements, the compass directions, and the *pa kua* forms an essential part of all feng shui practice. By knowing how each Element relates to the others, the feng shui practitioner is also able to interpret how the five Elements interact in the physical world to create good and bad luck.

The Elements are governed by two relationship cycles; the Productive Cycle and the Destructive Cycle. In the Productive Cycle the Element Water produces Wood, which in turn produces Fire, which produces Earth, which then produces Metal, which produces Water. The cycle is continuous with each Element mutually benefiting and generating the next in continuous harmony.

On the other hand the Destructive Cycle reflects the continuous process of decay that is prevalent throughout nature and is just as important as the Productive Cycle. In this cycle Wood breaks up Earth, which in turn absorbs Water, which puts out Fire, which melts Metal, which then comes back to chop down Wood.

Understanding the relationship between these two cycles helps feng shui practitioners to introduce individual Elements symbolically in homes and workplaces and to make changes in the emphasis of one or another Element, thereby changing the overall balance of energies that exist in the home or office.

Using the Elements in your home

The Elements, in particular, form an important part of our understanding of how to harness beneficial *ch'i*, since decorative items symbolizing the different Elements can enhance the relevant sector of the home.

When looking at the *pa kua* it becomes apparent that the five Elements do not divide evenly into the eight Aspirations so that some of the Elements have two compass directions. Earth represents Southwest and Northeast, Metal the West and Northwest, and Wood the East and Southeast. Water has only the one compass direction of North as has Fire which represents the South. But the Elements which appear twice—Earth, Wood, and Metal—are actually divided into a main Element direction and a lesser Element direction.

▲
The Element Earth relates to the Southwest and Northeast, and is represented by yellow, beige, and brown.

▼
The Element Wood links to the East on the compass and its color is green.

The Element Water is found in the North and its related colors are blue or black.

The Element Fire is found in the South and its color is red. The Element Metal is situated in the West and its colors are white, gold, and silver.

enhancing colors

Each of the five Elements is symbolized by one, two or three colors. Wood is green; Fire is red; Water is black or blue; Earth is brown or yellow; Metal is white or gold or silver. Using these as dominant colors for the various corresponding corners is part of practicing good feng shui. So using dominant green for the East and the Southeast, dominant red for the South, dominant black or blue for the North, dominant yellow for the Southwest and Northeast, and dominant white or metallic for the West and Northwest keeps your base colors to the correct Element.

Other colors can be used by following the Productive Element cycle. For example, in the East and Southeast, which are Wood, the Water colors of blue and black are excellent alternatives. This is because Water produces Wood. White or metallic colors are not good to use in the East or Southeast as Metal destroys Wood in the Destructive Cycle. For the Southwest and Northeast which are Earth corners, all shades and combinations of red will be excellent as Fire produces Earth in the Productive Cycle. The taboo color is any shade of green as Wood is said to destroy Earth.

The West and Northwest are Metal corners. Here, in addition to white, all shades and combinations of yellow, beige, and brown will be excellent as Earth produces Metal. Avoid red here as Fire melts Metal.

For the North, which is Water, white is excellent because Metal produces Water. And for the South which is Fire, green is good as Wood feeds Fire.

The Element theory of colors in interior decoration can be supplemented by other considerations. For example, the color red is usually considered auspicious, and the color purple is exceedingly lucky when combined with silver since these two words sound like money (*ngan chee*) in Chinese.

fire

The power of fire has filled people with awe for thousands of years and its strength is given full recognition in feng shui practice.

The Element of Fire is associated with the South and the season of summer. It is symbolized by lights, candles, and the color red. So by placing a bright light in the southern sector of your home you can enhance your personal fame and recognition, which is particularly beneficial if you happen to work as an actor, singer, politician, or writer, or indeed if you are involved in any profession that requires public recognition.

Fire is a very positive, *yang* energy and decorating rooms with red objects and bright lights increases fire energy, and is especially useful for people who are born in an Earth year because in the Productive Cycle of the Elements, Fire produces Earth. However, conversely, it would not be beneficial for someone born in a Fire year to have too much of the Element Water in their home in the form of fish tanks or fountains, because in the Destructive Element Cycle Water destroys Fire.

► **A red chair can add some positive *yang* energy to your living area.**

◄ **Light up the Southern sector of your home to boost your personal fame or enhance your recognition.**

► Drinking from vibrant red glass tumblers can be very auspicious, particularly for people born in Earth years.

▲ You can energize the Fire sector of your living area with items such as this red sofa.

earth

The Earth Element can be used in the home to restore harmony and balance in your life. You can achieve this by choosing ocher furnishings and symbolic earthy materials to decorate your rooms.

Earth interiors should be warm and soothing so that they induce closeness and togetherness, which is perfect for improving marital and relationship prospects. Such decor also stimulates knowledge or learning, and will be particularly helpful if your children happen to be studying for exams because they aid concentration.

The areas of life that are associated with Earth are Relationships and Marriage (Southwest) and Education and Knowledge (Northeast). To enhance these sectors in your home, you can introduce ceramics, terra-cotta items, or crystals, placing them in your Southwest and Northeast areas.

In the Productive Cycle of the Elements, Earth produces Metal. So the complementary Metal sectors of your home (West and Northwest) can also benefit from Earth furnishings. You can

place crystals, for example, in the West, which is associated with children. Adding Earth accessories to the Northwest, which is conducive to networking, can create new, exciting prospects in your life.

► **Ocher ceramic items can be placed in the Southwest to encourage good relationships.**

► **Placing china in the Northwest area of your home can help to bring about good networking prospects because Earth produces Metal, the Element of this sector.**

▲

Place porcelain items, such as these jars, in the Northeast of your home to promote your Education and Knowledge sector.

▼

The wonderful earthy colors of this terra-cotta stick figure can help to bring harmony to your home.

▼

Eyecatching ceramic bowls can be placed with crystals in the West to boost your Children corner.

metal

The materials that we use to decorate or furnish our homes affect the nature of the *ch'i* energy that is always circulating throughout every room. The surface and texture of the object also has some influence on the flow of *ch'i*. As a rule, hard, flat, shiny surfaces, such as metal, encourage *ch'i* to flow faster therefore making Metal a very positive, *yang* Element. The areas that are connected with Metal are Children (West) and Mentors and Networking (Northwest). So if you want to encourage the wellbeing of your children, want to get pregnant, or need to boost your networking connections in these parts of your home, you can place crystals or metal items such as picture frames, metal ornaments, or clocks here.

Sometimes it is also appropriate to place some *yang* metal objects in a predominantly *yin* area to create a more harmonious balance of the *yin* and *yang* energy.

Metal objects also help to "create" Water because in the five Elements Productive Cycle, Metal produces Water. So this area, North, which is linked to the Career Aspiration, will also benefit from the addition of some attractive Metal ornaments.

▲
These silvered pears catch the light and make a beautiful table decoration.

◄
Putting metal objects in the Northwest of your garden will encourage good networking prospects.

◄ Placing candles with metal candleholders in the West sector of your living room will encourage pregnancy or boost the welfare of existing children.

▼ The hard, shiny surface of metal objects such as this coffee pot can create positive energy in the kitchen area.

▼ You can also use metal objects, such as these watering cans, to enhance the West (Children) corner of your garden.

▲ Silver plates look stunning on the dinner table, and they will add some uplifting energy to any meal that is eaten off them.

water

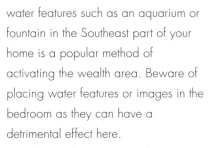

Ch'i energy is always circulating around the home and garden, and the flow of *ch'i* is also influenced by the elements, particularly water. Water is therefore a very powerful tool in feng shui practice, constantly moving, carrying, and accumulating *ch'i* throughout the surrounding environment.

The sight and sound of clean, naturally flowing water is both relaxing and soothing, but it can also be used to energize specific areas of your life and your home.

The area that Water is associated with is Career (North) so water features can be placed here to help with your career aspirations. Water is also the symbol of wealth, so placing

water features such as an aquarium or fountain in the Southeast part of your home is a popular method of activating the wealth area. Beware of placing water features or images in the bedroom as they can have a detrimental effect here.

Too much water is not, however, to be advised, because it can sometimes swamp or over-activate different sectors of the home. The bathroom, for example, is always viewed negatively by the Chinese because of its stagnant energies and due to the fact that water, linked to money, is constantly draining away from this area.

▲
Drinking water is an essential part of your inner feng shui, to balance and harmonize body energies.

◄
Water features in the garden are very auspicious. The ideal position for them is on the left-hand side of the front garden looking out from the front door.

▲
The flow of water, particularly rivers, is likened to the flow of *ch'i* and is considered beneficial by feng shui practitioners.

◄
Water is an important aspect of feng shui, but too much in the home can create an energy imbalance.

▲
Positioning aquariums in the Southeast part of your living room can enhance your wealth prospects.

wood

The element Wood is not simply a large piece of timber. As one of the five Elements, it evolves from *yin* and *yang* and represents all living trees and plants that exist.

The sectors associated with the Element Wood are Wealth and Prosperity (Southeast) and Family and Health (East). So if you need to boost the overall family finances or want to promote the general wellbeing of your family, place some wooden items plus some energizing plants and flowers in the Southeast corner and the East of your home. Hardwood items are *yang* whereas softwood ones are *yin*, so balance the placement of them carefully to create the right harmony.

If you were also born in a Wood year then it would be very sensible for you to emphasize any items that are symbolic of Wood. Alternatively, you can use a water feature, such as an aquarium or water fountain, to strengthen the Wood sector of your home, as the Water Element generates Wood in the Productive Cycle. Wood also produces Fire, so the complementary Fire area of the home (South) will benefit from wood accessories.

► Wooden bowls are very versatile accessories that look equally good on a coffee table or being used for a meal.

◄ Lamps with wooden bases add a mellow, appealing warmth to any room.

▼ Interestingly carved wooden items can be placed in the living room in your Eastern corner.

▼ Attractively grained wooden serving utensils can add interest to the dinner table.

► Wooden chairs in stunning designs such as this one can become a focal part of any room.

► Wooden benches can add interest in a garden and can boost your Wealth corner in the Southeast.

▲ Wooden containers can hold pens or pencils and enhance your Family and Health sector in the East.

Feng shui enhancements
the aspirations

Each of the eight trigrams that are part of the *pa kua* (see pages 26–29) relate to an Aspiration that is associated with an area of your life in a specific section of your home.

To help your life work more smoothly or to improve one aspect of it, a section can be "activated" by using its Element to enhance that particular Aspiration, for example the trigram for the North is *K'an*, its Element is Water and it relates to Career, the South's trigram is Sun and is associated with Wealth and Prosperity. "Cures" can also be strategically positioned to energize or boost that particular sector of your home.

Career

Trigram: *K'an*
Area: It is associated to the North sector of the *pa kua* and the same area in your home
Element: Water. This is symbolized by water features, including fountains, fish aquariums and the colors blue and black

To promote your career, energize the Career corner of your office and home. If your bedroom is in the North, a very *yin* area, then activate the North of your living room (see Tips).

Looking after your luck
A good location for your home study is

ENERGIZING YOUR CAREER
tips

❍ Always sit in an office facing the door so that you don't get caught unawares.

❍ Make sure your desk faces your personal Best Direction (see pages 76–77).

❍ Sit with a solid wall behind you, rather than a window, or you will always feel that you lack support.

❍ At business meetings, sit facing the door in one of your personal Best Directions.

❍ *Specifically for the North corner:* Use water features such as aquariums or small water fountains to activate this area.

❍ Use fish, ideally vigorous guppies in an aquarium no more than 2ft (61cm) long, to produce *yang* energy.

❍ Use appropriate Metal symbols as this Element feeds Water in the Element Productive Cycle.

❍ Add a symbolic small blue light to this area.

the Northwest which favors luck. It is linked to metal, so place hollow metal wind chimes here or hang a picture of a large mountain to symbolize the Element Earth, which produces Metal in the Productive Cycle.

Desktop energy

Use your compass to check your home or office desk's orientation, then place it facing your Best Direction (see pages 76–77). If possible leave the floor in front of your desk empty for a mini "bright hall" effect. Put fresh flowers on the East side for yang energy, and a small healthy plant on the Southeast to enhance your prospects for a good income and personal growth.

A round crystal in your desk's Southwest corner will help work relationships.

Clear papers and files as they create too much yin energy, and clutter will cause stagnant ch'i. Watch out for the sharp edges of tables and desks shooting "poison arrows" at you and reposition furniture to avoid them.

Wealth and Prosperity

Trigram: *Sun* (a Chinese trigram, not the sun in the sky)

Area: It is attributed to the Southeast sector of the *pa kua* and the same area in your home

Element: Small Wood. This is symbolized by plants, flowers, and the color green. It really represents all growing vegetation.

This area is one of the most important in your home as it represents your family's wealth and prosperity. By boosting this area you can encourage prosperity and financial security for all members of your family.

However there can be detrimental factors. A toilet, for example, located in the Southeast sector is not good for wealth. If there is one try to minimize the effect by keeping the toilet seat down and the door shut when it is not in use. This will help to limit the amount of positive energy being flushed away.

Good office space

The Southeast sector of the house is excellent as an office if you work from home. In the garden, the Southeast corner can be activated by planting plenty of green plants and keeping them healthy as their wellbeing symbolically indicates the current state of your wealth.

Also, adding a water feature or fish pond to the garden in the right place will help keep the energy in harmony. Make sure, though, that it is in proportion to the rest of the garden.

BOOSTING WEALTH tips

❍ Place a healthy plant in your wealth area in the Southeast. Plants with sharp leaves or thorns, such as cacti, should not be used. The money plant—the jade plant—is excellent for this area as it symbolizes wealth.

❍ Use water features as Water produces Wood in the Element Productive Cycle. A small feature with trickling water and some plants, or an aquarium with nine fish (an auspicious number) would greatly activate this area.

❍ If the wealth area is dark, attract positive energy by placing a lamp with a low-wattage bulb in the area and keeping it on all of the time.

❍ Placing a mirror on a dining room wall to reflect the food on the table is very auspicious as it symbolizes the "doubling of wealth."

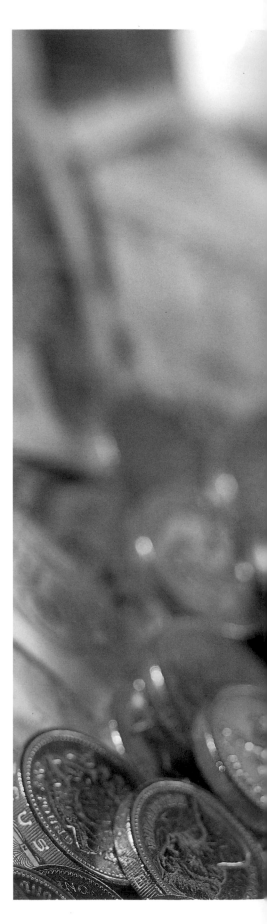

Relationships and Romance

Trigram: *K'un*

Area: It is linked to the Southwest sector of the *pa kua* and the same area in your home

Element: Strong Earth. This is symbolized by crystals or paired items such as hearts or candles, and the color yellow

If you feel that an existing relationship is in the doldrums or you can't find the ideal partner, then use feng shui principles to make improvements.

Enhancing family ties

The formula for activating the Southwest sector can be applied to the home as a whole or simply to the sitting room. However, do not activate the Southwest sector of your home if it includes the toilet or kitchen as these rooms have very different connotations when situated here.

To enhance family relationships, make sure you have photographs of your family displayed as well as of your husband or wife in the Romance corner. Ornaments for this area should always be in pairs to symbolize togetherness (see Tips).

Boosting your love life

Sometimes a relationship which has gone well for a long period hits difficulties. Look and see what has changed—especially if you've just moved house as you may need to make adjustments in your new property to restore the balance.

CREATING PERSONAL HAPPINESS

tips

Do

❍ Activate the Southwest sector of your home, living room, or bedroom with real or silk red flowers such as roses—a potent symbol of love.

❍ Use crystals to attract *yang* energy to this sector.

❍ Display paired items such as mandarin ducks, double fish, butterflies, or footsteps of Buddha.

❍ Enhance the Southwest sector with figurines or statues of couples, ideally lit by a table lamp with a ceramic or terra-cotta base.

❍ Use a light in this sector of your living room to draw on the complementary Fire energy as Fire feeds Earth in the Element Productive Cycle.

❍ Display a picture or fan featuring a red peony flower on the wall of your bedroom.

❍ Hang a two or nine rod crystal or ceramic wind chime in the Southwest corner of your living room to increase your popularity.

Don't

❍ Have an aquarium or basin in your bedroom.

❍ Use live plants or flowers in the bedroom as they are too *yang*.

❍ Hang pictures of single people in your home.

If you are single and can't find the right relationship, again look at your home. Perhaps you have too many pictures of single people and a dormant or stagnant Relationship sector with clutter in it.

Remember no amount of money can buy you love, but by following a few simple feng shui tips, you can improve the prospects of bringing love into your life.

Health and Family

Trigram: *Chen*
Area: It is attributed to the East sector of the *pa kua* and the same area in your home
Element: Strong Wood. This is symbolized by healthy, thriving plants, and a deep green color

Good health can be getting the balance right in various aspects of your life and home, but having good health is the best basis from which to improve and expand your life.

A healthy balance

In Chinese cuisine ingredients are combined to balance the *yin* and *yang* qualities of food which keeps the *ch'i* balanced and moving inside the body. *Yang* foods are considered "hot or fiery" and beneficial to the elderly, while the young can eat more *yin* or "cold" food.

Enhancing your health

Good feng shui in this area of your home, living room, or garden represents good health for the family. Placing a healthy round-leaf plant in the East is very auspicious (see Tips). Nurture it, and replace it if it withers. Lifelike green artificial plants, to signify Spring the season of the East, can also be used.

Pictures of plants, especially bamboo and plum flowers, can also be placed in the East if there is no room in that area for a potted plant.

Auspicious feng shui of the East is of paramount importance as good health is the very essence of life and is to be treasured.

GOOD HEALTH tips

○ Try to arrange your bed so that your head points in your Health (*tien yi*) Direction when sleeping (see pages 76–77).

○ Place a healthy green plant without sharp leaves in the East.

○ To promote good health make sure that the center of your home and living room is uncluttered.

○ Boost the East with a complementary water feature, as Water feeds Wood in the Productive Cycle.

○ Display an image of *Sau*, the God of Longevity, one of the Three Luck gods (*Fuk Luk Sau*) in a special place in your home.

○ Place a symbolic painting of peaches, the symbol of immortality, in the East, or use ceramic items or ornamental jade trees which have lucky number of six or eight peaches.

○ In the Eastern corner of your garden, use a sculpture of a pair of cranes, a symbol of long life, especially if it is displayed near bamboo or pine trees—other signs of longevity.

○ Place a dragon-head tortoise at the back of your home for general support and good prosperity.

Children

Trigram: *Tui*

Area: It is linked to the West sector of the *pa kua* and the same area in your home

Element: Metal. This is symbolized by statues made of metal and electrical appliances such as TVs and stereos, and the color white

Children represent our hopes for the future and in Chinese society to have descendants to carry on the family name is paramount, and children are often referred to as "precious jewels." Filial piety is expected of children and they are expected to look after their parents throughout old age.

Children and family harmony

By activating the West sector in a living room or a home (see Tips) you will promote family harmony, enhancing the chances of having children. If you already have children, when this sector is boosted it will influence the whole psyche of the offspring, affect their health, behavior and also their academic performance.

On the adverse side, though, unfavorable feng shui here can make children behave in an unruly way, cause bad communication with parents, and bring about unmotivated and poor academic performance at school.

The Chinese have numerous symbols for fertility, and in fact many Chinese homes display the Family Buddha—a Happy Buddha carrying many children in his arms. This god is supposed to bring "Descendant Luck." Chinese marital bed sheets and pillow cases are often made in auspicious red or pink colors with embroidery of the auspicious dragon and phoenix on them to ensure a fertile union.

tips

TO IMPROVE FAMILY OR CHILDREN OR LUCK

○ The matriarch of the house should sleep in her *nien yen* or Family Luck orientation according to her *kua* number in the Eight Mansions Formula (see pages 76–77).

○ Place metallic objects or ornaments like hollow wind chimes and brass bells in the West sector.

○ Use Earth items such as crystals, glassware, ceramics, and terra-cotta as Earth produces Metal in the Element Productive Cycle.

○ To motivate children in their studies, place natural quartz or amethyst crystals in their work area.

○ Always sit your child (children) to face his/her *fu wei* or Self-improvement Direction (see pages 76–77).

○ To inspire your children's academic ability, hang a picture of a well-known genius, such as Einstein or Isaac Newton, in their study.

○ Use white, gold, or silver objects or fabrics in the West of the family's living room.

Education and Knowledge

Trigram: *Ken*

Area: It is associated with the Northeast sector of the *pa kua* and the same area in your home

Element: Small Earth. This is symbolized by crystals and the colors yellow or brown

Many Chinese families consider scholastic achievement as a prerequisite to a life of excellence and status. So, in the modern world today, feng shui can play a very important part in enhancing scholars' Education Luck.

Activating your education area

When being educated or training for a skill or profession, this is a vital sector to activate. To activate Education Luck, use a compass (see pages 78–79) to find the Northeast sector of the living room or bedroom of the student In the Productive Cycle of the five Elements, the Fire Element produces Earth, so objects associated with Earth, such as ceramics or lights with Fire are therefore good enhancers of this area (see Tips).

However, avoid using metallic lamps with sharp or angular shapes in the Northeast as *sha ch'i* or bad energy will emanate from the angles. You can also place empty ornamental terra-cotta or ceramic urns here. These are believed to be able to store auspicious *ch'i*.

Symbols for a successful scholar

The most potent feng shui symbol of scholastic and career achievement is the *yee mun lung* or Dragon Carp sign—a carp emerging from a dragon gate and transforming into a dragon. They are sometimes displayed in pairs above the entrance of some Chinese homes, and are said to inspire the glory and bravery of the dragon in the residents of the home—especially when they go out to work.

Today education is as pivotal to a successful career as it was in the past—knowledge is still power.

EDUCATION SUCCESS tips

○ Energize the Northeast corner with natural or man-made crystals.

○ Enhance the area with rounded-shaped lamps with ceramic, terra-cotta or glass bases.

○ Introduce some red in the Northeast to strengthen and feed the Earth Element as Fire produces Earth in the Productive Cycle.

○ Cultivate a respect for educational materials. Do not put text books on the floor or step on them.

○ Display academic achievements like diplomas or certificates with pride on the Northeast wall of a study.

○ Do not put plants or metallic ornaments like bells or wind chimes in the Northeast.

○ Position your desk in the Northeast sector of a room or study.

○ Arrange your desk to face your *fu wei* or fourth Best Direction (see pages 76–77). This will help to tap your inner Knowledge Luck.

Fame

Trigram: *Li*

Area: It is connected to the South sector of the *pa kua* and the same area in your home

Element: Fire. This is symbolized by any light, candles or fire, and the color red

Fame comes in many forms in the Chinese culture. It means acknowledgment of a person's talent by a higher authority, often the employer, combined with an honorable reputation and recognition in society and among your peer group.

ACTIVATING FAME tips

○ Place lights, candles, and red ornaments in the South sector of your home or living room. In the garden area, put plants with red leaves or flowers in the same sector.

○ Use chandeliers or lamps with a round base, with red, white, or yellow light bulbs. Avoid *yin* colors such as blue here.

○ Hang a lead-faceted crystal tied with a red string by the window to bring in *yang* sun energy and attract inspiring rainbow colors into the room.

○ Auspicious paintings of birds, with strong red coloring, such as the phoenix, roosters, or flamingoes are particularly auspicious in the South for Fame Luck.

○ Build a fireplace in the South of a room to kindle the Fire Element and Fame.

○ Wooden objects will benefit Fame in the South as Wood feeds Fire in the Productive Cycle.

○ Do not put a painting depicting water in the South as Water destroys Fire in the Element Destructive Cycle.

○ Avoid a swimming pool in the South as this could bring disaster, particularly to the family head as Fame Luck will be destroyed by "big water" in the pool.

○ Hang a red picture of sunrise in the South to inspire new beginnings.

The brilliant South

The South represents Fire, brightness and happiness, the sun and vibrant summer *yang* energy. It is symbolized by vermilion red which the Chinese use during celebrations such as weddings or birthdays.

In modern times, fame by recognition of a person's skill contributes to anybody's success. There is nothing more rewarding than for an employee's work to be acknowledged by the boss. A home

with a southern Fame corner (in the home or living room) that is well lit with *yang* energy and auspicious enhancements (see Tips) will bring the residents external recognition of their achievements. Family members may be promoted at work or enjoy an increased business turnover. It will encourage high self-esteem, boosting their morale so that they can achieve their goals. It is important to get right as bad feng shui in this sector will bring the opposite.

Mentor Luck

Trigram: *Ch'ien*

Area: It is associated with the Northwest sector of the *pa kua* and the same area in your home

Element: Strong Metal. This is symbolized by metal and objects such as hollow metal wind chimes and the colors white, silver, and gold

The Chinese believe that Mentor Luck forms the backbone of a person's success and good fortune. Having a mentor is regarded as the key to attainment and power in society.

Attracting good Mentor Luck

This area is placed above all the other Aspirations by the Chinese as it is considered particularly fortunate to have such luck. To attract good Mentor Luck, it is imperative to ensure that feng shui in the relevant sector is well activated. If this sector is blessed with good feng shui, the head of the household will enjoy good career prospects. As this area is ruled by the Metal Element, placing metal objects in this corner will help to enhance Mentor Luck.

A powerful tool to use in this sector is a six-rod hollow wind chime which summons abundant positive energy. A wooden wind chime would not work here as the Metal Element destroys Wood. The Fire Element, in the form of lights, should not be placed here either, as Fire destroys Metal in the Destructive Cycle of the Elements and would diminish your Networking Luck. This is a good corner for hi-fi systems or TVs as

electrical items are considered to be of the Metal Element.

With a balance of *yin* and *yang* energy and auspicious feng shui in the Northwest sector of a home, householders will cultivate mentors and other helpful people in their lives who will help them to achieve the success they desire.

❍ Enhance your Mentor Luck with metal objects in this corner—TV sets, hi-fi systems, metal ornaments or pictures of mentors in silver frames.

❍ Earth objects such as natural crystals, lucky crystal fish or frog ceramic or clay ornaments are equally potent in this corner as Earth supports Metal in the Element Productive Cycle.

❍ Religious objects or artefacts can be placed here to attract divine Mentor Luck.

❍ Chinese deities like the *Kuan Kung* (the god of Protection and Prosperity), the laughing Buddha or *Fuk, Luk* and *Sau* (the gods of Three Lucks) enhance Mentor Luck.

❍ Boost the Mentor corner with six Chinese coins tied with red ribbon or a six-rod wind chime—auspicious, traditional feng shui objects.

❍ Paint this area using white or metal colors—silver or gold—or use the colors in your soft furnishings or furniture. Do not use red (Fire) or green (Wood) as these clash with Metal.

Crystals

Crystals are now a very popular feng shui cure and can create significant shifts in the flow of energy in a space or a room. They can work alongside other enhancements to boost one of the eight Aspirations of the *pa kua* in your home (see pages 26–29). They can prove to be very powerful so it is important to treat them with respect. If you use too many, choose too large a size, or put them in the wrong place, more harm than good can be done. Clear the room of clutter before you hang a crystal (see pages 18–21) because they expand energy and you don't want to increase the difficulties you already have which might be symbolized by having too many unwanted items.

Crystal energy

A sparkling crystal hanging in a window can spread a beautiful rainbow of colors across the walls and transform a space. One of the key principles in feng shui is to keep energy or *ch'i* moving and vibrant since stagnant *ch'i* is unhealthy. Clear, faceted crystals expand and lift *ch'i* and have an extraordinary capacity to activate energy. One small sphere hanging in a window can have a dramatic effect on a room, especially when it catches the sunlight, and it can add a powerful charge to a particular part of the *pa kua*, the energy map of your space.

If you want to enhance a particular aspect of your life, hang a crystal in the window relating to the appropriate part of the *pa kua*. The light refracting through the cut-glass like a prism will bring a symbolic boost or charge of energy to the corresponding part of your life. Choose the area significant for Wealth and see how the crystal impacts positively on your bank balances or opportunities. Place one in the window of your Relationship area and see your current partnerships become more harmonious.

Hanging a crystal

Hang the crystal toward the top of the window in the center of the pane of glass suspended from the wood above by a neat pin or nail. Position it a short distance away from the glass. A 20mm sphere is normally sufficient for a small room, while a 30mm should be adequate for most average-sized rooms. Hanging crystals may also be used to break up any negative *sha* coming through a window from a T junction, a lamp post or an offending tree.

USING OTHER CRYSTALS

tips

❍ A natural quartz or an amethyst crystal can be used to boost the Northeast—Education and Knowledge section of your home or living room.

❍ A cluster of natural quartz can help to energize the Relationship area of your home in the Southwest.

❍ Rose quartz is a very healing stone that is associated with romance. It can be placed in a disruptive teenager's room to calm them down.

❍ Amethyst is a very powerful crystal. It can be placed in a sick person's room to aid their healing.

❍ Cleanse your crystals when you first buy them from a crystal shop by holding them for a short time under running water. This will help to remove any negative energies they may hold.

❍ Hanging crystals can be cleansed monthly by dipping them in some fresh spring mineral water. Set your intent for your crystals' purpose when you first hang them, and renew it every time you clean them.

Using
pa kua cures

The *pa kua* symbol is a very ancient and powerful Chinese symbol dating back many thousands of years. It contains eight trigrams which are said to contain the mysteries of the universe with profound meanings and interpretations (see also pages 26–29).

Each trigram is linked to a compass direction—the four cardinal points, North, South, East, and West, and the four corners, Northeast, Northwest, Southeast and Southwest. They are also associated with the eight life Aspirations which relate to different aspects of your life such as career or wealth and prosperity (see pages 42–57).

When it has been laid over your home, according to the eight house Aspirations formula for activating feng shui luck, each sector of the *pa kua* can be activated by a different Element and hence type of "cure," which when used will increase the particular luck that is associated with that area.

Southeast—Wealth and Prosperity—Small Wood

Cure: Water fountains.

Why: The Wealth and Prosperity Aspiration is represented by the Element Wood, and in the Productive Cycle of the Elements Water produces Wood. So if you place a water fountain in the Southeast of your home, a room, or garden you will attract some Wealth Luck.

Where: Use a water fountain in the Southeast of your study, living room, or garden. It is not recommended that water features be used in the bedroom.

South—Recognition and Fame—Fire

Cure: Lights—any kind of electric light, candle or fire.

Why: Lights, used throughout the home signify *yang* energy, but also symbolize the Fire Element.

Where: Lights can be installed in in the South sector of the home, a room or garden. They can be hung from the ceiling, mounted on the wall, placed on table tops as lamps or used as uplighters. When using lights in the South sector make sure that the base and lampshades are brown or green (Wood Element), or red (Fire Element). Don't use blue fittings or bases (Water Element) because in the Element Destructive Cycle Water destroys Fire.

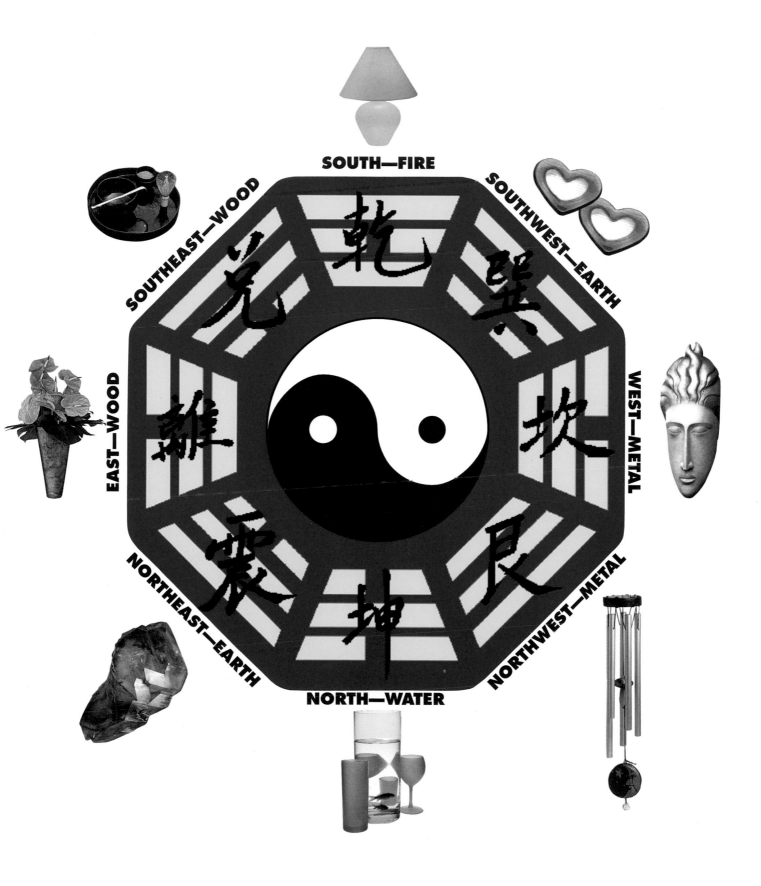

SOUTH—FIRE

SOUTHEAST—WOOD

SOUTHWEST—EARTH

EAST—WOOD

WEST—METAL

NORTHEAST—EARTH

NORTHWEST—METAL

NORTH—WATER

Southwest—Marriage and Romantic Happiness—Strong Earth

Cure: Symbolic pairs of items such as two hearts, Chinese double happiness characters, or pairs of candles. If they are red, so much the better.

Why: The color red symbolizes passion and is also associated with the Element Fire which, in the Productive Cycle of Elements, produces Earth, the ruling Element of the Marriage and Romantic Happiness Aspiration. Putting two objects together signifies a happy couple whereas one object symbolizes being single or alone, and three or more objects symbolize too many people being involved in the relationship, possibly even suggesting marital affairs.

Where: Ideally, placing two red candles or two red hearts in the Southwest area of the bedroom will energize the Marriage and Romantic Happiness Aspiration. They can also be placed in the Southwest sector of the living room.

West—Children—Metal

Cure: Metallic statues, electrical appliances—TV and stereo.

Why: TVs and stereos represent the Element Metal which is associated with Children. Using metal objects in the West sector of your home increases your children's chances of enjoying happiness and applying themselves to their studies. Enhancing this area also works just as well if you are trying to have children.

Where: Place your TV and stereo system in the West sector of your living room. Putting *yang* electrical appliances of this sort in any other room, especially bedrooms (which are places of rest), creates bad feng shui as they produce an overabundance of *yung* energy in the Five Element Destructive Cycle.

Northwest—Mentors and Networking—Strong Metal

Cure: Hollow metal wind chimes.

Why: To attract influential friends and mentors activate the Northwest sector of your home. This area represents the Mentors and Networking Aspiration and is associated with the Metal Element. Metal wind chimes give off attractive tinkling sounds, allowing *ch'i* to rise and circulate through the home.

Where: Hang wind chimes so they catch the breeze easily. Attract Mentors and Networking Luck by hanging them in the Northwest location, or alternatively you can place them in the Northwest area of the garden, study, or the living room.

North—Career—Water

Cure: Fish tank or other water feature.

Why: The ruling Element of the Career sector is Water. Enhance this area by placing a fish tank here with goldfish in it in a combination of either eight or two gold and one black fish as these are symbolic, auspicious numbers. The movement of the fish creates abundant *ch'i* and excellent conditions for attracting Career Luck.

Where: Place the fish tank in the Northern area of your living room or study but avoid putting water in the bedroom. Don't go overboard and introduce a very large tank, because too much water can effectively "drown" your prospects.

Northeast—Education & Knowledge—Small Earth

Cure: Crystals—natural quartz crystal, amethyst or a handmade lead crystal paperweight.

Why: The Education and Knowledge Aspiration, which is associated with Study Luck, is governed by the Element Earth. If anyone in your family or household is studying, you can place Earth objects, such as crystals, in the Northwest area and these will effectively focus the Element and benefit their studies. As crystals come from deep within the Earth's surface, they are excellent sources of Earth Luck.

Where: Focus on energizing the Northeast corner of the study or the room in which the student's desk is placed to bring Study Luck to the students in your family or household. Place the desk in the Northeast corner of the room with a crystal situated in its Northeast corner.

East—Family and Health—Wood

Cure: Indoor plants with rounded leaves—especially money plants. If you use cut flowers, make sure they are always fresh as dead flowers are *yin*.

Why: To keep members of your family fit and healthy and free of illness, it's recommended that the Family and Health Aspiration in the East sector of a room or home is activated by healthy, thriving plants—because plants are symbolic of Wood, the Element which governs this Aspiration.

Where: Place a money plant in the East sector of any main room in the home, especially the living room.

Balancing
your inner body energies

Feng shui balances and removes energy blockages in the home so that *ch'i* can flow freely, but there are other natural health disciplines that use the same theory to have the same effect on our bodies, helping to prevent or control illness. Chinese herbal medicine, acupuncture, acupressure, and shiatsu, in the same way as feng shui, use the Chinese *yin/yang* theory so that energy or *ch'i* is regulated in the body. *Tai ch'i* is a gentle martial art that encourages a good flow of *ch'i* by performing controlled movements in coordination with natural breathing and mental intent. Eating macrobiotic, ideally organic food, also helps to balance *yin* and *yang* in the body, nourishing both body and soul.

Chinese herbal medicine

Throughout human civilization people have noted different things which could be eaten for their medicinal properties.

The Chinese were among the first to document the effects of such natural remedies. Huang Ti—the Yellow Emperor (2,696 to 2,598 B.C.E.)—is reputed to have discovered herbal medicine and recorded his findings.

How it works

Chinese herbal medicine practitioners treat the body as a complex set of

◀ Sometimes several different herbs are mixed together to create the right Chinese herbal remedy for an individual.

▶ Different herbal potions to suit the individual's ailment are prescribed by a Chinese herbal practitioner.

energy channels. There are four significant factors that need to be taken into consideration when prescribing medicines: energy, blood, meridians, and internal organs. *Ch'i* flows along 12 energy channels, known as meridians, which are linked to the body's organs and form a circulatory system around the body. Six are considered to be *yin* and six *yang*. The internal organs are also influenced by the five Elements and the Harmony of the five Sentiments (Anger, Joy, Pensiveness, Sorrow, and Fear). To keep the body functioning well, it is necessary to keep all of the five Sentiments in balance. A Chinese herbal practitioner will also want to determine whether an illness is "hot" or "cold," "wet," or "dry." as this will affect which herbs it is necessary to prescribe for the patient's treatment.

Visiting a practitioner

When a patient visits a Chinese herbal practitioner he will do four examinations called *si jian*. The first covers lifestyle, diet, physical activity, and pain. Next he will study facial color, body type, the tongue, and mental state and expression. He will then listen to the patient's breathing, coughing, and voice and note their smell. Lastly, the practitioner will feel for three pulses in each wrist to see how the major organs are functioning and to check on the flow of *ch'i*.

Once the diagnosis has been made the practitioner will decide on the relevant herbal remedy. The two most popular forms of taking the preparations are in soups and tea. Chinese herbal medicine is believed to treat or alleviate diseases such as arthritis, asthma, depression, diabetes, and eczema.

Acupuncture

Acupuncture, literally "needle piercing" is an ancient healing therapy that has recently become popular in the West. It is part of Traditional Chinese Medicine (T.C.M.) which also includes Chinese herbal medicine, massage, and exercise systems such as *tai ch'i*.

How it works

In the same way that feng shui techniques manipulates the energy flow in a house, an acupuncture treatment will do the same in the body. Thin needles are inserted in specific points to stimulate the flow of energy—*ch'i*—and remove any blockages that may be causing health problems. To keep well the Chinese believe that the right balance of *yin* and *yang* energy is needed. So in acupuncture needles are inserted at points along 12 meridian (energy) lines which are believed to be connected to the body's main organs. Six meridians are *yin* and six are *yang*.

Visiting a practitioner

An examination by an acupuncturist will be similar to the one given by a Chinese herbal practitioner. He or she will ask about your lifestyle, diet, and medical history. He will also ask about your digestion, circulation, and emotions. Your tongue will be studied in detail, and your pulses will be taken. There are three on each wrist and he can test for up to 28 pulse qualities which relate to an organ or function. For treatment one or two sterilized needles can be used, but more often four to eight.

Acupuncture has been found to help ailments such as arthritis, back pain, stress, depression, and hay fever.

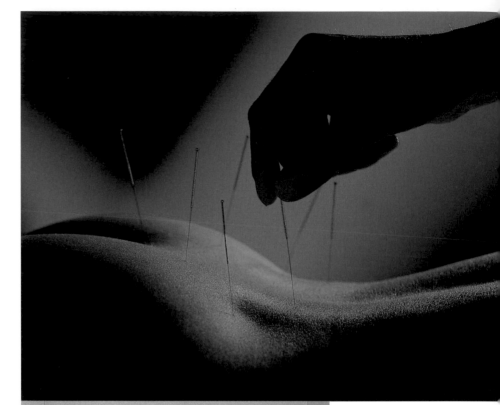

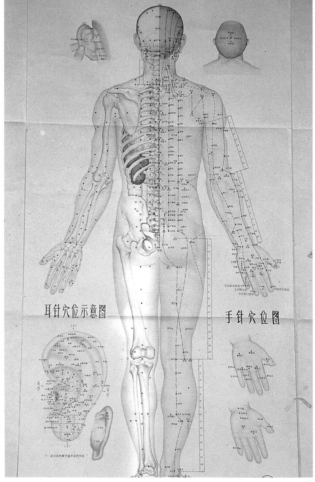

◄
In acupuncture 12 meridian lines contain many different points which are linked to different body organs. After diagnosis the acupuncturist will insert needles in chosen points to treat the patient's condition.

◄

In an acupuncture treatment sterilized needles, ½–1in (12–24mm) long are inserted at different points on the body to stimulate the flow of *ch'i* and to remove any blockages which may be disrupting a person's wellbeing.

Shiatsu

Shiatsu uses the same principles as other traditional Chinese healing systems. This involves an understanding of *yin* and *yang* (see pages 16–17), the five Elements (see pages 30–41), and an appreciation of how *ch'i* energy works and Oriental diagnosis. Shiatsu synthesizes this body of knowledge with a practical, and intuitive form of massage that has become very popular in recent years.

How it works

The purpose of shiatsu is to restore harmony and balance to the *ch'i* of the recipient. A skilled shiatsu practitioner can ascertain what the client needs to restore a sense of

harmony and wellbeing during a shiatsu treatment.

Visiting a practitioner

A shiatsu practitioner, like an acupuncturist, is taught to appreciate the causes of *ch'i* imbalance, such as emotional turmoil, or stress. By questioning a client and using Oriental diagnosis, the practitioner can find the areas and organs needing attention.

A shiatsu treatment usually lasts an hour with the client remaining clothed lying on a futon. After some limb stretching, the practitioner concentrates on points which can be released by thumb pressure. Shiatsu can help relieve stress and boost the immune system.

▼

A shiatsu treatment involves the practitioner pressing specific points around the client's body, which is normally fully clothed. Emphasis is placed on the lower abdomen, which is considered to be the body's center. Releasing tension here helps *ch'i* to flow out toward the arms, legs, the head, and the neck.

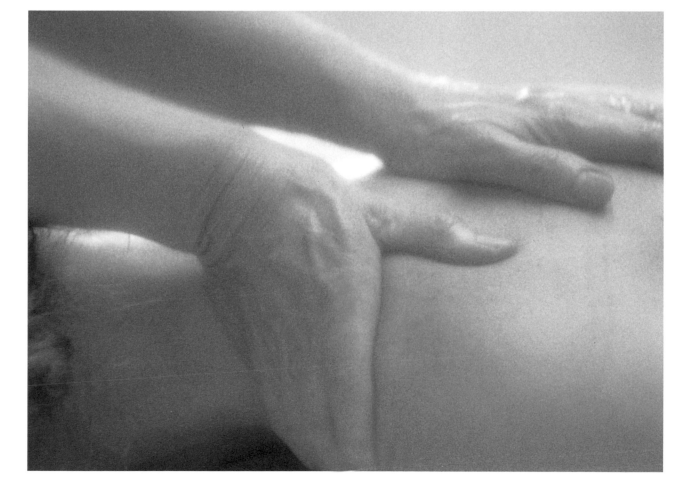

Acupressure

As humans we have instinctively pressed parts of our bodies to relieve aches and pains, so the simplicity of acupressure is that it brings a level of healing back within our own grasp.

How it works

It works like acupuncture with the principle that the body is charged by *ch'i* energy. This is channelled through 14 meridians with 379 acupoints that connect energetically with the function of our internal organs. When *ch'i* gets blocked it can cause stagnation.

Acupressure is a simple technique to learn from reference books and can be used for self-treatment. When treating points breathe out as you apply pressure, pressing down slowly until you feel a slight resistance. Hold for one or two seconds, then release as you breathe in. Ideally repeat five or six times.

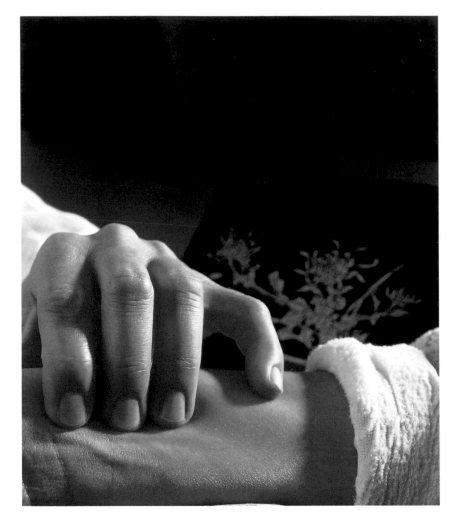

Tai ch'i chuan

This gentle form of martial art, in the same way as Chinese herbal medicine, acupuncture, and feng shui, is interconnected with the five Element theory and a belief in *ch'i* energy. The *tai ch'i* symbol is a visual representation of *yin* and *yang*, the opposing, yet inter-related energy forces.

The founder of *tai ch'i* is generally thought to have been a Taoist monk called *Chang San-Feng*. As the monks spent many hours sitting and meditating, it was felt they needed a special system of exercise which could loosen the joints and maintain the energy flow through their bodies.

Monks, regarded as peaceful and non-violent, were often the target of bandits, so it was therefore believed that they should be able to defend themselves, but be able to do this without showing apparent violence or aggression.

How it works

On its simplest level *tai ch'i* is a health exercise. However, it is not what might usually be regarded as "exercise." One of the principles of Traditional Chinese Medicine (T.C.M.) is that there are meridian lines which travel through the body carrying *ch'i* energy. *Tai ch'i chuan* promotes the smooth flow of this energy by performing specific,

controlled movements in coordination with relaxed, natural breathing and the application of *yi*, which is the intent or focus of the mind. Performing a set sequence of *Tai ch'i* exercises stimulates the free flow of *ch'i* through all the channels or meridians that exist in the body.

Apart from promoting the flow of *ch'i* energy, *tai ch'i* also helps to increase flexibility and suppleness of the joints and exercise various muscle groups. The smooth, gentle movements also aid relaxation, enabling the person to keep their mind calm and focused. These benefits can prove to be very useful in today's hectic and very stressful society.

◄
Acupressure is a simple technique that can be used for self-treatment. Thumb and finger pressure is used to stimulate different acupoints all over the body.

►
Fresh, seasonal, local fruit such as apples should form 5% of your daily macrobiotic diet. Always try to buy organic produce wherever possible.

▼
Tai ch'i is a gentle martial art which combines controlled movements, relaxed breathing, and mind intent to stimulate the flow of *ch'i*.

Inner feng shui

Feng shui techniques can help to balance and harmonize your environment, but you also need to think about the balance of *yin* and *yang* in your inner body.

The wholefood cuisine of macrobiotics was developed about 100 years ago in Japan. It encourages you to live in harmony with your environment by eating seasonal, indigenous produce, balancing *yin* and *yang* foods, activity with rest and taking time to meditate.

The ideal diet

To regain your inner wellbeing, eat this macrobiotic diet daily for a month:

❍ Use up to 50% cooked wholegrain cereals, such as short-grain brown rice and barley millet.

❍ Use up to 25% local and seasonal vegetables—half root and half green.

❍ Use 10–15% protein. Good sources are herring, sardine, cod, sole, haddock, well-cooked beans such as azuki or chick peas, plus soya products.

❍ Eat a bowl of Japanese *miso* soup (A dish with.kelp seaweed, vegetables, and *miso*).

❍ Use 5% fresh, local seasonal fruit.

❍ Drink spring water, fresh carrot and apple juice and cereal-based coffees.

H A R M
your home with feng shui

The home is our haven where we can retreat from the pressures of the outside world. It should be a calm, pleasant environment where the energy (*ch'i*) flows freely through each room without encountering any harmful obstructions. By learning basic feng shui placement skills, how to use enhancements, and the best use of color, lighting, textures, or fabrics you can create balance and perfect harmony in all your living areas.

- How to feng shui your home
- The entrance and hallway
- The living room
- The dining room
- The kitchen
- The bathroom
- The bedroom
- The children's bedroom
- The garden

How to
feng shui
your home

Feng shui affects every aspect of your life and the way it is applied in your home can be both beneficial and detrimental to the way you live and your surrounding environment.

In the West, feng shui is not a science, as its principles cannot yet be proven by scientific method. It is not a religion, although some of its advocates may consider it part of their religious practice. It is not just a philosophy as it also encompasses many practical tools and techniques. It is not a belief system: asking someone if they believe in feng shui is like asking them if they believe in the weather. It's not a question of faith but a fact of life.

The underlying principle of feng shui is to live in harmony with your home and environment so that the energy surrounding you works for you rather than against you. By harnessing the positive forces of *ch'i*, enhancing different sectors of your home and placing cures against negative forces you can create a positive, balanced atmosphere for yourself. This will work if you live alone, with a partner, or with your family.

The eight Aspirations

One feng shui formula concerns the eight main life Aspirations. These are divided into eight sectors, and each of these sectors corresponds to a

particular compass direction: Wealth and Prosperity—Southeast, Recognition and Fame—South, Marriage and Romantic Happiness—Southwest, Children—West, Mentors, Helpful People or Networking—Northwest, Career Prospects—North, Knowledge and Education—Northeast, Family Relationships and Health—East (for more information on the Aspirations see pages 42–57).

Each of these Aspirations corresponds to the eight directions of the *pa kua* (see pages 26–29), which is one of the most basic feng shui tools.

▲
By applying feng shui methods to your home you can improve its energy flow which will benefit all who live there.

Once you have laid the *pa kua* over your home and identified where the particular Aspirational locations are, you can then energize them using a number of different cures and enhancements (see pages 60–63). This will stimulate the positive flow of *ch'i* and help to create some good feng shui for you.

related subjects

Feng shui, or something similar, is practiced in China, Hong Kong, Taiwan, Singapore, Malaysia, and in Chinese-speaking communities all over the world. Similar practices occur in Tibet, Vietnam (*phong thuy*), the Philippines, Indonesia, Bali, Thailand (*hong sui*), Japan, Hawaii, and India (*vaastu shastra*).

Environmental radiation

When considering feng shui placement, as well as *ch'i* energy, it is important to consider the occurrence of natural and artificial electromagnetic energy, which can affect the health of those who encounter it. Unstable or disrupted naturally occurring electromagnetic radiation, emanating from the earth, can create harmful effects called geopathic stress.

Man-made electromagnetic fields are generated by electrical equipment such as computers or televisions in our homes and offices, and these should be kept to a minimum in the home.

Dowsing

This technique enhances the understanding and effectiveness of feng shui. Among other things, dowsing may be used to detect *ch'i* and earth energies and perhaps to help choose and devise feng shui cures.

Bau-biologie

This is a German theory about the effects of so-called "black streams" which are supposed to cause illness in those who sleep or work in their vicinity.

▲
Using feng shui in the home will benefit all the family members.

◄
Enhancing your home's Wealth corner can help to improve your career prospects and overall prosperity.

►
Hanging lead crystals are a useful feng shui enhancement.

Schools of feng shui

Feng shui has been around for thousands of years. It reached its first golden era in the fourth century C.E. Over many centuries different schools of feng shui have developed. Each school has a slightly different approach to the subject, although the basic principles remain the same. The following is just a very brief introduction to the different schools of feng shui thought.

Form School

This school of feng shui focuses on the environment, concentrating on the contours of physical landscapes, their shapes, size, and watercourses, and the relationship between the physical

formations and a dwelling. The four directions of the compass are symbolized by four animals. The East relates to the green dragon, the West the white tiger, the South the red phoenix and the North is the black turtle or tortoise. Nestled between these you may find the most auspicious location for a house or a village. The Form School is also concerned with straight alignments which produce undesirable, so called, "poison arrows" which create *sha ch'i*.

Traditional Chinese Compass School

The Compass School uses the eight trigrams of the *I Ching*, the eight-sided

pa kua symbol, and the *lo shu* magic square (used to divide up the house or office into nine sectors). These tools are used to diagnose the feng shui quality of locations and the *ch'i* flow coming from different directions.

This type of feng shui originated in China over 3,000 years ago, with the first definite text mention in 220 B.C.E. It was based on a scientific, formulaic approach to feng shui which is thousands of years old. A usual practice is for the Career sector of the eight trigrams to be oriented to magnetic North.

Black Hat Sect (B.H.S.) feng shui

A more recent school of thought which is widely practiced in the U.S.A. is

◄

Depending on the school of feng shui that is used the orientation of the living room will vary. The Compass school will take a specific reading from the front door, whereas the Black Hat sect say that the front door always faces the Career sector.

► Feng shui also applies to gardens, and the relevant areas will benefit from being enhanced with metal objects or statues.

◄ Incense appeals to the senses and creates a pleasant aroma in a living area, helping to lift the energy.

Black Hat Sect (B.H.S.) feng shui or "Black Hat Sect Tantric Buddhist" feng shui. Developed in the U.S.A. 15 years ago by Thomas Lin Yun, it is a hybrid of Tibetan Buddhism, Taoism, and feng shui which has been simplified for Western tastes. It has a huge cult following, particularly in the U.S.

With this school of feng shui, rather than using the traditional magnetic compass or *lo p'an* to determine directions, each house or room is judged from the position of its door.

B.H.S. feng shui states that the main door to each room faces the Career sector. This may result in adjacent rooms or houses having apparently contradictory directions.

This type of feng shui has been popular in America since 1986. It is based on a more spiritual approach to feng shui. The eight trigrams on the

pa kua are known more colloquially as the *bagua*.

Intuitive feng shui

There is much talk about "intuitive feng shui." However, feng shui, which has its own set of rules, can no more be

considered intuitive than either geography or physics. Individual practitioners may be more perceptive than others, but feng shui changes must be based on the established rules and not just perceptive feelings that the consultant may have.

Personal Directions

Before you start to look at the feng shui in your home, it is important to learn about the Directions which are auspicious for you as an individual and this can be done by working out your *kua* number.

Your *kua* number determines your Best Directions, the four possible directions which you should face while doing the most fundamental things—for example, you should sleep with your head pointing to your most auspicious Direction (or *sheng ch'i*). The eight Aspirational locations (see pages 26–29) always remain the same, whatever your *kua* number is, but it is important to orientate your chair and the head of your bed to correspond with one of your individual auspicious Directions.

Calculating your *kua* number and your Best Directions

To determine your Best Directions (for sleep, study, and eating) it is necessary to calculate your *kua* number using the following steps:

1 If you are born between 1st January and 20th February then you will have to check the date on which the Chinese (Lunar) New Year fell in the year of your birth (see table opposite). If you were born after 20th February, proceed immediately to Step 2. If you were born before the Chinese New Year, you should subtract one from the year of your birth. For instance, if you were born on 6th February 1964 (when Chinese New Year fell on 13th February) you should count your birth year as 1963.

2 Take the last two digits of the year of your birth and add them together. For example, if you were born in 1974, then add 7 and 4 to give 11. If the result is greater than 9 add the digits together, e.g. 1+1=2.

3 If you are a male, subtract this answer from 10, e.g. 10 – 2=8. If you are a female, add 5 to the number produced in Step 2, e.g. 2 + 5=7.

4 If the number is bigger than 9 then add the digits together again.

5 If the answer is 5 and you are male, use *kua* number 2. If you are female and the answer is 5, use *kua* number 8.

6 The result is your *kua* number. Now use this *kua* number to find your Best Direction or sheng *ch'i*.

Kua **Best Direction**

1	Southeast
2	Northeast
3	South
4	North
6	West
7	Northwest
8	Southwest
9	East

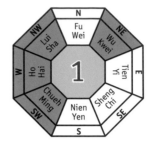

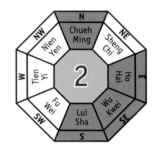

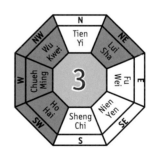

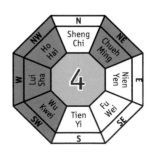

Chinese (Lunar) New Year Calendar 1924–2005

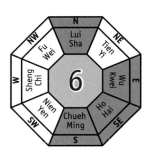

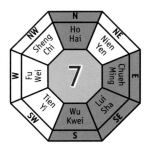

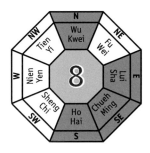

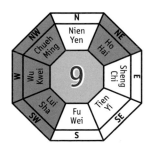

Year	Chinese year starts in	Year	Chinese year starts in
1924	Feb 5th	1965	Feb 2nd
1925	Jan 24th	1966	Jan 21st
1926	Feb 13th	1967	Feb 9th
1927	Feb 2nd	1968	Jan 30th
1928	Jan 23rd	1969	Feb 17th
1929	Feb 10th	1970	Feb 6th
1930	Jan 30th	1971	Jan 27th
1931	Feb 17th	1972	Feb 15th
1932	Feb 6th	1973	Feb 3rd
1933	Jan 26th	1974	Jan 23rd
1934	Feb 14th	1975	Feb 11th
1935	Feb 4th	1976	Jan 31st
1936	Jan 24th	1977	Feb 18th
1937	Feb 11th	1978	Feb 7th
1938	Jan 31st	1979	Jan 28th
1939	Feb 19th	1980	Feb 16th
1940	Feb 8th	1981	Feb 5th
1941	Jan 27th	1982	Jan 25th
1942	Feb 15th	1983	Feb 13th
1943	Feb 5th	1984	Feb 2nd
1944	Jan 25th	1985	Feb 20th
1945	Feb 13th	1986	Feb 9th
1946	Feb 2nd	1987	Jan 29th
1947	Jan 22nd	1988	Feb 17th
1948	Feb 10th	1989	Feb 6th
1949	Jan 29th	1990	Jan 27th
1950	Feb 17th	1991	Feb 15th
1951	Feb 6th	1992	Feb 4th
1952	Jan 27th	1993	Jan 23rd
1953	Feb 14th	1994	Feb 10th
1954	Feb 3rd	1995	Jan 31st
1955	Jan 24th	1996	Feb 19th
1956	Feb 12th	1997	Feb 7th
1957	Jan 31st	1998	Jan 28th
1958	Feb 18th	1999	Feb 16th
1959	Feb 8th	2000	Feb 5th
1960	Jan 28th	2001	Jan 24th
1961	Feb 15th	2002	Feb 12th
1962	Feb 5th	2003	Feb 1st
1963	Jan 25th	2004	Jan 21st
1964	Feb 13th	2005	Feb 9th

A step-by-step guide

This is a practical guide on how you can apply the principles of feng shui to enhance your home and life. Use it as a checklist as you start to implement feng shui practices in your home.

STEP 1

Stand at your front door and look outward. See if you can identify any large structure or object pointing toward you, generating what feng shui refers to as "secret arrows." These can be a neighbor's satellite aerial, a row of telegraph poles marching down the street, a church spire, or a long straight road aimed at your front door. If any of these generators of "secret arrows" appear to be pointing at your front door you should deflect their baleful influence by placing an eight-sided *pa kua* mirror over the front door, facing outward. But be careful where it faces as negativity can be sent toward your neighbors. Do not use *pa kua* mirrors inside the house, ever.

STEP 2

Repeat the same process as in Step 1 to check the back door and all your major windows.

STEP 3

Using a compass, and standing again in your front door, determine the direction that your house faces. You can use an ordinary orienteering compass or an elaborate Chinese *lo p'an*, but make sure that you align the North pointing end of the needle with the Northern point of the compass

card. (If you do not have a compass you may be able to work out the "facing direction" of your front door from a street map.) Note this down for later comparison with your personal Best Directions.

STEP 4

Examine your entrance way and make sure that nothing blocks the smooth flow of *ch'i* through your front door or in the hallway. Any clutter and other obstructions immediately inside or outside your door should be removed. If possible the path from your gate to your front door should curve, to let *ch'i* meander in.

STEP 5

Sketch a floor plan of your home and place a *pa kua* diagram over the floor plan of your home to match its compass points (see pages 26–29).

STEP 6

Ascertain which of the eight Aspirations listed on the *pa kua* you wish to improve or energize. If, for example, you choose to energize the prosperity sector which is in the Southeast area, look at the *pa kua* and you will discover that the Element associated with the Southeast is Wood. To stimulate this sector you need to place Wood (i.e. growing plants) in that area. Alternatively, you can energize that corner with the Element Water which helps "produce" Wood in the Element Productive Cycle (see also pages 30–31).

A word of warning, do not try to energize too many sectors at once or you may find that you are overwhelmed by all the opportunities that come your way!

STEP 7

If your home is not a square or rectangular shape, check the outline floor plan of your home to see if there are any missing corners. By missing corners we mean a sector on the *pa kua* which does not correspond to a room or part of a room. This might occur if your home is L-shaped, for example. If you feel the Aspiration associated with this sector is important to you then you should "create" it by using mirrors. Full-length mirrors placed against the wall of adjoining rooms will appear to "fill in" the room space that is missing.

STEP 8

Check your kitchen. Make sure that your food preparation area does not involve you or your partner standing with your back to the door. If it does, try to reorganize the kitchen so that the door is visible from where you usually stand at the main food preparation area. Ensure that there is no Element conflict between the Elements Fire and Water in the kitchen. In other words ensure that your stove (Fire) is not directly facing or confronting either your sink or fridge (Water). If it does then try to relocate it. Finally, check the direction of the "mouth"—the source of your gas or electricity—of your stove (hob and oven) to see that it faces ideally in one of your Best Directions (see Step 13).

► When you have mapped out your home using a compass and the *pa kua* you can decide which areas to energize. Your living room, for example, may be in the South—your Fame and Recognition area.

◄ Hallways should always be kept neat and tidy and free of clutter. This is to allow *ch'i* to enter freely and meander through all the rooms in the home.

▲ The kitchen is an important place in the home as it is here that nourishment is provided for all the family.

STEP 9

Check the lounge and/or dining room. Try to make sure that any mirrors in the dining areas reflect the food on your table to "double your prosperity."

STEP 10

Check your bedroom. Make sure that nothing is suspended above your bed or threatens you subconsciously, such as overhead built-in cupboards or hefty pictures above the bed. Ensure that you can't see yourself in any mirror when you are in a sitting position in your bed. If so, either move the mirrors, cover them up, or angle them away from the bed. Make sure that the head of the bed has a solid support behind it, and that it is not located under a window.

STEP 11

Check the location of your toilet and bathroom. This is important because these rooms are the areas where water exits from your home. Work out if they are in any of the eight sectors of the *pa kua* which you consider important, for example a toilet in your Southwest sector will impact on your relationships. The reason for this is that these rooms flush water out of the house and this tends to carry with it the beneficial *ch'i* energy. For example, if your toilet or bathroom falls in the Western quarter it will therefore flush away your children's luck. This might be critical for you if your children were having a difficult year, or be of no importance whatsoever if you did not have children. If these "wet rooms" fall in a sector that is important to you, then try to keep the door closed and the toilet

seat down, or even go one step further and cover the door of the "wet room" with a full-length mirror to "make the room disappear."

STEP 12

Check your garden, if you have one, and apply the *pu kua*, using a compass, to a plan of your garden. Make sure that any paths do not lead straight, like arrows, to your doors as this can cause *sha ch'i*. When you are a little more advanced with feng shui techniques you might consider installing a pond or water dragon, although the correct positioning of this is critical. Having attended to the locations in

your house and garden, you now need to look carefully at your personal directions. These are specifically beneficial for you and should influence how you decide to position all the moveable furniture within all the rooms in your home.

STEP 13

Calculate what your *kua* number is using the method that is detailed earlier on pages *76–77*. Then write down on paper your Best Direction (*sheng ch'i*) and also your other three Best Directions: your Health Direction, your Family Direction, and your Mild Good Fortune Direction.

◄
A path that curves gently through a garden simulates the flow of *ch'i*, which always travels in in a curving motion.

▲
A round dining table is considered to be one of the most auspicious shapes in feng shui.

◄
A bathroom drains away a lot of positive *ch'i* because of the constant water flow. However, it can be made into a pleasant and relaxing environment.

STEP 14

Orientate your bedhead to face your *sheng ch'i* or Best Direction. If this is not possible then choose one of your other three Best Directions so that your head points in that direction. If you have health problems for example you should orientate the head of the bed in your Health Direction. Of course it is unlikely that both partners sharing the same bed will have the same Best Directions. In this case, the rule is that for a happy marriage the woman's Best Direction takes precedence, although you could decide with your partner which Best Direction should be used.

STEP 15

Orientate your working direction. Try to make your desk chair face your *sheng ch'i* Direction if you have a home office. Extend this to your business or office if you can possibly manage it. But make sure that your working position does not leave your back to the door of your office. It is more important to have the door to your office where you can see it rather than have your chair facing your *sheng ch'i* Best Direction.

STEP 16

Orientate your eating direction or dining room seating to your *sheng ch'i* Best Direction.

These are the basic feng shui changes to improve the energy in your home, but much more detailed information on each living area is given on the following pages in this section. Don't make too many changes at one time as the effects can be powerful, but do things gradually and then watch for the positive results.

▲
A large hallway
can also contain a
small office, but
remember to keep
it tidy or you will
impede the flow of
ch'i coming into
the house.

▶
You can liven up a
dull hallway with a
carefully planned
display of
interesting prints.
Experiment with
different-sized
frames until you
get the type of
arrangement that
you want.

▼
Bright color
schemes can lighten
up a dark and
narrow hallway.

▶
This hallway is
very welcoming to
visitors because of
its light and airy
appearance.
Clutter-free, it also
encourages *ch'i* to
enter freely.

The
entrance
and
hallway

First impressions really do count when it comes to your home's entrance and hallway. It is a gateway to the rest of the home, it is not only where we enter and leave but also where we greet and say goodbye to guests. The hallway is consequently the first and last area of the home that other people see—how it looks and feels leaves a lasting impression on visitors.

It also has the power to influence the quality of feng shui in the entire home. It should be clutter-free, bright and uplifting, exuding a warm and welcoming ambience, yet be practical enough to withstand the busy comings and goings of everyday life. It is the main area of dispersal for *ch'i* energy after it enters the home through the front door, which is why it is so important that it can make its way unhindered by too many items here.

By painting the hallway an airy, light color, featuring bright fabrics and colorful floorcoverings (see Style File), and using mirrors to expand it, where necessary, you can make it a pleasant and inviting place to enter. Be careful, however, where you place the mirrors as they are an important feng shui tool.

The flow of *ch'i*

Ideally, *ch'i* should always be allowed to flow smoothly and evenly through the front door, into the hallway, and from there disperse into each room in your home.

Hallways vary from home to home but they can be quite narrow, cold places, sparsely decorated with little furniture to add any charm—in fact just the sort of area where *ch'i* could rush through unabated.

Also if a hallway is cluttered with too many items, or if it contains sharp, angular objects, the flow of *ch'i* will be hampered and the rest of the house will then suffer. A balance has to be sought

here to encourage a smooth and even flow of *ch'i*.

Slowing down the energy

One typical problem occurs in the hallway if the back door of the home is directly in line with the front door. Unless the flow of *ch'i* is slowed down, the hallway will act like a wind tunnel—*ch'i* energy will simply rush through the front door and straight out the back without circulating through or accumulating in the home.

You can slow down this flow of *ch'i* by hanging a windchime from the ceiling of the hall, or place a piece of furniture or a potted plant against the wall to encourage the *ch'i* to take a more meandering route.

The location of the stairs also has great significance to the feng shui of

▲
Hallways do not have to be bland or dull. Plan the decor carefully and add accessories such as seasonal flowers to lift the energy.

The ideal entrance and hallway

A hallway needs to be bright and welcoming. Also use a mirror to widen the space, but never hang it opposite the door as it will send the *ch'i* out again.

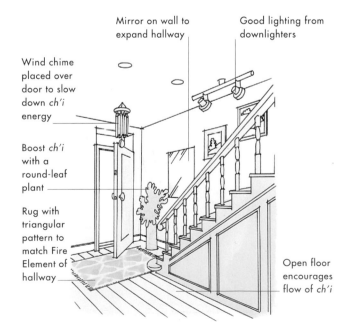

Wind chime placed over door to slow down *ch'i* energy

Boost *ch'i* with a round-leaf plant

Rug with triangular pattern to match Fire Element of hallway

Mirror on wall to expand hallway

Good lighting from downlighters

Open floor encourages flow of *ch'i*

tips

○ If your hallway is a very narrow place a mirror on one of the walls to expand it. However, do not put it directly opposite the front door.

○ Place inspiring art pictures and attractive landscapes on the walls.

○ Decorate the hall in a light, inviting wallpaper or paint to draw people in.

○ Make sure the hallway is well lit with pendant lighting or tracks of spotlights. Avoid dark corners by utilizing accent lighting.

○ If the kitchen is open-plan and can be seen from the front door, either put a door on it or screen it off with plants.

○ Your stairs should always be solid, if not fill in the gaps between the treads as otherwise you may find that you start to lose some of the family's savings.

the hallway. A front door that opens directly onto the stairs allows *ch'i* energy to rush up the stairs or enter right into the heart of the home without being dispersed or moderated, which can prove harmful to all the occupants. To avoid this, circulate and slow down the flow of *ch'i* by placing some windchimes at the foot of the stairs or over the front door.

A cluttered hall

Too much clutter in the hallway also encourages the accumulation of stagnant, negative *ch'i*. If the clutter is in a central position then the effect on the occupants may be to make them feel depressed and it can also influence their overall health and general wellbeing. Remove any unnecessary furniture or objects—

► **Think about the decoration scheme in the hall carefully, as it is here that everybody enters your home and gets the first impression of you and your family.**

▲ **The entrance to your home should be wide and inviting. Placing a mirror on a side wall can help to visually increase the width.**

walking into a bundle of coats and brollies or tripping over shoes and bags as you walk through the door is also annoying and irritating.

Creating a light space

Make sure the hallway is always light and tidy, brightly decorated and has enough space to move freely. You can stimulate the flow of *ch'i* by introducing a healthy plant and lighting it well.

style file

Rugs

Rugs offer perhaps one of the easiest ways to transform a hallway. In feng shui terms, by simply using certain colors or patterns you can help activate a healthy energy flow into and through your entrance area. Laid casually over a large wooden or ceramic floor, rugs help to highlight specific areas of the hall, adding interest and color to what might otherwise be a bland, rather dull area.

From kilims to dhurries and from needlepoint to rag rugs, choose colors that will help enhance the correct Element of the hallway. For example, if your hallway is situated in the South

and you wish to maintain the ambient Fire *ch'i* energy there, pick out rugs with hues that contain some fiery reds and oranges. Since rugs can form a very large part of the surface area of the hall, the color, texture, and pattern is very important as it may have a dominant effect on the overall decorative scheme.

Also think carefully about the type of pattern you choose as large patterns, deep shades and borders will make a hallway's width look smaller, while small patterns, light colors, and plain surfaces will increase the impression of available space.

▼
This rug, predominantly black and gray in colour, is ideal for a hallway that faces North as these colors support the Water Element. The circle pattern is also supportive of this Element.

◄

Bold, colorful stripes on a rug can make a dramatic impact in a hallway, but always choose a pattern that will blend in with your color scheme and which won't dominate too much.

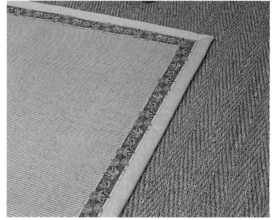

▲

Take time to choose the design of your rug for the hallway, as big or small patterns can give the impression of reducing or increasing the hall's width.

◄

Traditional rugs, often made in Asia, contain complicated patterns with different symbols and shapes. Try to match these and their colors to the Element of your hall to encourage in some more beneficial energy.

▲
Arrange seating harmoniously around a coffee table to create a focal point for visitors. It can also help to stimulate conversation.

The living room

The hub of family life, the living room is a place to receive and entertain guests as well as being an area in which to relax and unwind. It is the public face of our private homes. A multifunctional space, it is usually one of the largest rooms in the home and plays an important role in family life. It's here where we sit and relax, receive visitors, show off our possessions and display our decorative taste. Sometimes the same room has an integral dining area or some of the space may be used as a home office.

With many diverse activities carried out in the living room, it is particularly important that it enjoys good feng shui as this will affect the wellbeing of all its occupants. Ideally, it should be located at the front of the house, near the main door so that it benefits directly from the strong flow of *ch'i* energy that enters the house. This is also the best room in which to activate and make use of the eight life Aspirations (see pages 42–59) because everyone uses this room.

The living room should be comfortable to be in, have good lighting, comfortable chairs (see Style File) and a warm and inviting color scheme.

▲
A yellow and red color scheme immediately makes a living room appealing to all new visitors.

►
Warm, wooden floors help to prevent *ch'i* from stagnating in a living room, while candles and a fire boost energy.

Relaxation zone

The living room should be clutter-free and not over-furnished. Store away books and magazines neatly, and arrange furniture so people can easily move through the room without bumping into anything. *Ch'i* energy will stagnate in a room that is cluttered and people will find it difficult to relax in such an environment.

Photographs of friends chatting and laughing and family portraits will further enhance the sense of cohesion. Sharp-edged furniture and ornaments should be avoided as their corners will produce harmful *sha ch'i* and hamper the flow of *ch'i* through the room. Soften any such sharp edges, such as exposed shelves, with some seasonal flowers or green plants, for example, or decorate a square table with a tablecloth.

Different-shaped rooms

If the room is L-shaped, one approach is to demarcate it with furniture to "square it off," and then treat it as two separate rooms. For example, you can keep one section as a formal area to receive guests and then use the other part as a family room. Another way is to fill in the "missing corner," perhaps by

placing a mirror on the wall so the missing corner appears to be there, work out the central position to hang it from using the shape of the "completed" room.

Comfortable sitting

Seating is perhaps one of the most important items of furniture in the living room and how it is arranged affects the ambience of the entire room. Sofas and armchairs should preferably be rounded in shape and comfortable to sit on.

Try to arrange seating around a focal point such as a coffee table or a fireplace to stimulate interesting conversation, but avoid placing seats so their backs are facing the door as people sitting in them can feel subsconsciously threatened.

People are automatically drawn to the warmth and light of an open fire. Not only does it energize the entire room, but it creates a cosy, welcoming feel which is important to any living room. Don't place seating under a structural beam as people will suffer from the *sha ch'i* that comes down from it. Look out for any sharp corners in the room that could emit "poison arrows." If there are any, soften them with plants or furniture.

The ideal configuration of the furniture in the room should simulate the octagonal shape of the *pa kua*. This

► **Pastel colors can be pleasing on the eye in the living room. Soft shades also help to make the room feel and seem bigger.**

○ A water feature will boost favorable *ch'i* in the living room. A correctly placed indoor waterfall or a fish tank stocked with goldfish will help to energize the room.

○ Sharp objects, such as swords and knives or dead animal trophies should not hang on the wall as they generate negative energy.

○ Avoid table lamps or ornaments with sharp edges as they can generate cutting, *sha ch'i* in the room.

○ Plan your room so that *ch'i* energy can flow uninterrupted in a curved motion through the room. Watch out for corners where energy can stagnate and keep them free of clutter.

○ Furniture should be solid not flimsy, and sofas and armchairs should have high backs for comfort and to symbolize support in life.

○ Natural quartz, amethyst, or a lead-faceted hanging crystal plus ceramic or terra-cotta vases can be placed in the Northeast section of the room to boost Education Luck.

arrangement would inspire a warm and harmonious ambience as the chairs will be in conversation range of one another, which encourages good interaction among all the occupants of the home.

Seating that is used for long periods—such as when someone is reading or watching television—should be placed so the occupant is facing one of their personal Best Directions. This is determined by their *kua* number (see pages 76–77).

Color

Using wall coverings in subtle colors such as cream or yellow will make the room appear and feel bigger. Shades of yellow are ideal here as they also stimulate conversation and promote sociability and harmony with all the family members.

The color of the living room can be chosen to emphasize the feng shui changes that you have made. Ideally you should choose the room's color to

▲
Chairs with soft, fluid lines will not obstruct energy flow.

▼
A living room should not be over-furnished and have minimal clutter to let *ch'i* energy flow unimpeded. Avoid sharp edges that cause *sha ch'i* or conceal them with bushy plants.

The ideal living room

TV away from seating area to reduce electromagnetic stress

High-back sofas and chairs give comfort and support, arranged for sociability and good flow of *ch'i*

Uplighters for *yang* energy

Inspiring picture to give psychological boost

Stripped wood floor supports tree energy and boosts *ch'i*

Pure wool rug for *yin* energy and comfort

Curved edges on unit prevents cutting *ch'i*

▲

High-back chairs give support, but don't place them with their backs to the door as people sitting in them will feel uncomfortable.

◄

Fresh flowers can energize a living area, but always change them regularly as when they die they become *yin*.

relate to its location in your home's plan. So, for example, if it is located in the Southwest or the Northwest of the home then it should be a shade of yellow to relate to the Earth Element.

If it is in the Southeast or East it should be green because of the Wood Element.

North and South positions would benefit from shades of blue and red respectively. Rooms in the Northwest and West areas can be effectively enhanced by shades of white, silver, or gold, which all represent the Metal Element.

Getting rid of negative *ch'i*
Televisions, which are so often the main focus of living rooms, should be covered and hidden when they are not in use as the electrical field that emanates from them has a negative effect on the energy of the room. But this effect can be minimized by strategically placing plants in front of it to absorb the bad energy.

▼
Colorful, ethnic cushions can create a cosy atmosphere in a living room and make the seating more comfortable.

Curtains

You can control the flow of *ch'i* and natural light through your living room windows with anything from the most luxurious velvets to the sheerest of muslins. Try fully draped curtains in *yin* hues of porcelain greens and powdery blues or go for bolder, *yang* shades such as spicy tangerine or fuchsia.

To give your window the type of treatment it deserves, first you need to consider its architecture, function, and the amount of natural light you require.

Think about privacy, the location, and most importantly the flow of *ch'i*.

Curtains are a good solution as you can use virtually any material from velvets and damasks to linens, silks, cottons, and muslins. The weight of the fabrics will affect the *ch'i* energy entering the room through the window. If this needs slowing down or inhibiting then opt for heavier fabrics, particularly for rooms that overlook busy roads. Curtains are great for softening the lines of a living room, introducing wonderful textures, and filtering light.

▲
Heavier fabrics can help to slow down the passage of *ch'i* through a living room window that looks out onto a busy road.

▶
Light, flowing curtains allow more natural light into a darker, more *yin* room.

◄

Patterned, silky, Indian-style fabrics can add a flowing, sensuous feel to a living room. Choose *yin* or *yang* hues that harmonize with the existing color scheme of the room.

▲

Big curtains in *yin* shades of powdery blue can be used to balance stronger, more powerful *yang* elements in a living room.

▼

Extravagantly draped curtains can complement the style of the window frame. This rolled design is also ideal in the West of the room as its curved shape represents Metal.

Chairs

Comfortable, attractive chairs are an important part of the living room and need to be chosen carefully. Simple and commodious shapes invite you to lounge and provide an island of privacy for napping, contemplation, or some quiet reading.

When you select chairs for the living room think about materials, shapes, and colors. Wooden chairs are particularly beneficial in the Southeast and East, while metal chairs are good accent pieces in the West and Northwest. Curvaceous chairs or chairs upholstered with fabric denoting curves and circles are fluid and organic and stimulate sociability. If you want to soften a square living room, choose chairs with exaggerated proportions, ones that are voluptuous and moon-shaped as they denote movement and are more symbolic of the natural world and the cycles of nature. For good sociability, any seating should be arranged so that it forms a balanced shape such as a circle, octagon, or square which in feng shui terms promotes happy and harmonious relationships.

►

The fluid shape of this chair encourages relaxation and comfort. Placed in the South of the living room its red color will help to enhance your Fame corner.

► A comfortable blue armchair can be positioned in the North of your living room to stimulate your Career corner.

► Metal chairs can help to boost the West and Northwest corners of your living room.

▲ When chairs face the middle of the room, they allow different seating directions to suit both friends and family.

◄ Curvaceous chairs will always help to stimulate sociable interaction when they are placed in the living room.

▲ You can calm down a loud decorating scheme in a living room with chairs in neutral colorways such as this soft biscuit shade.

FENG SHUI

style file

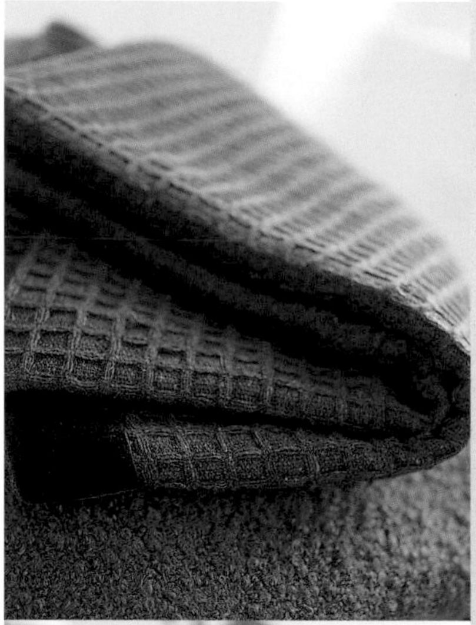

►
Textured blankets are soft and warm to touch. They have very *yin* qualities and make luxurious, soft throws on sofas.

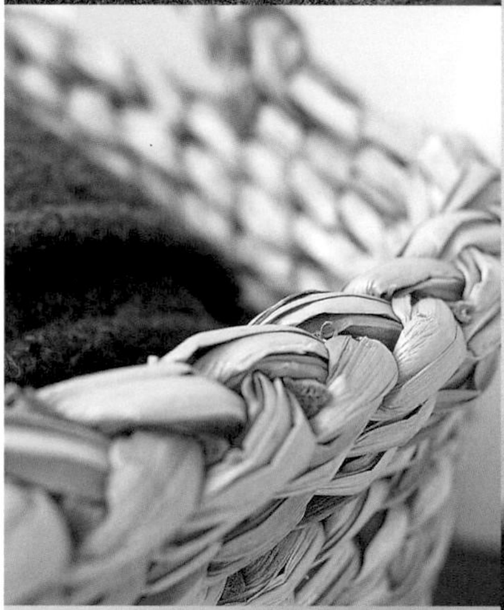

►
Natural fibers, like the wicker basket shown here, have *yin* qualities and need to be mixed with some other *yang* objects.

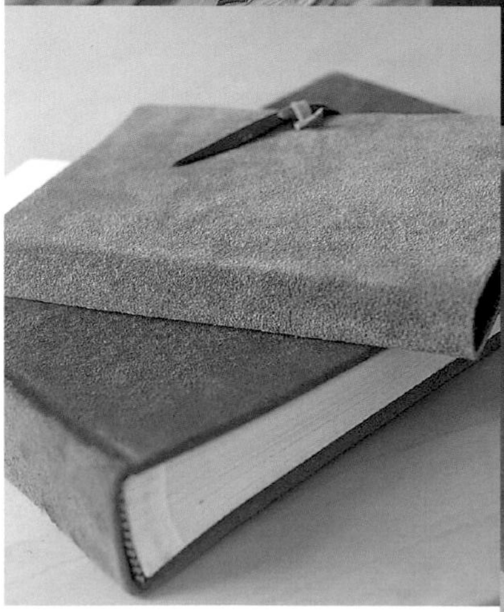

►
Always remember to balance textures in the living room. Place these leather-trimmed books on a hardwood table or next to some ceramic items.

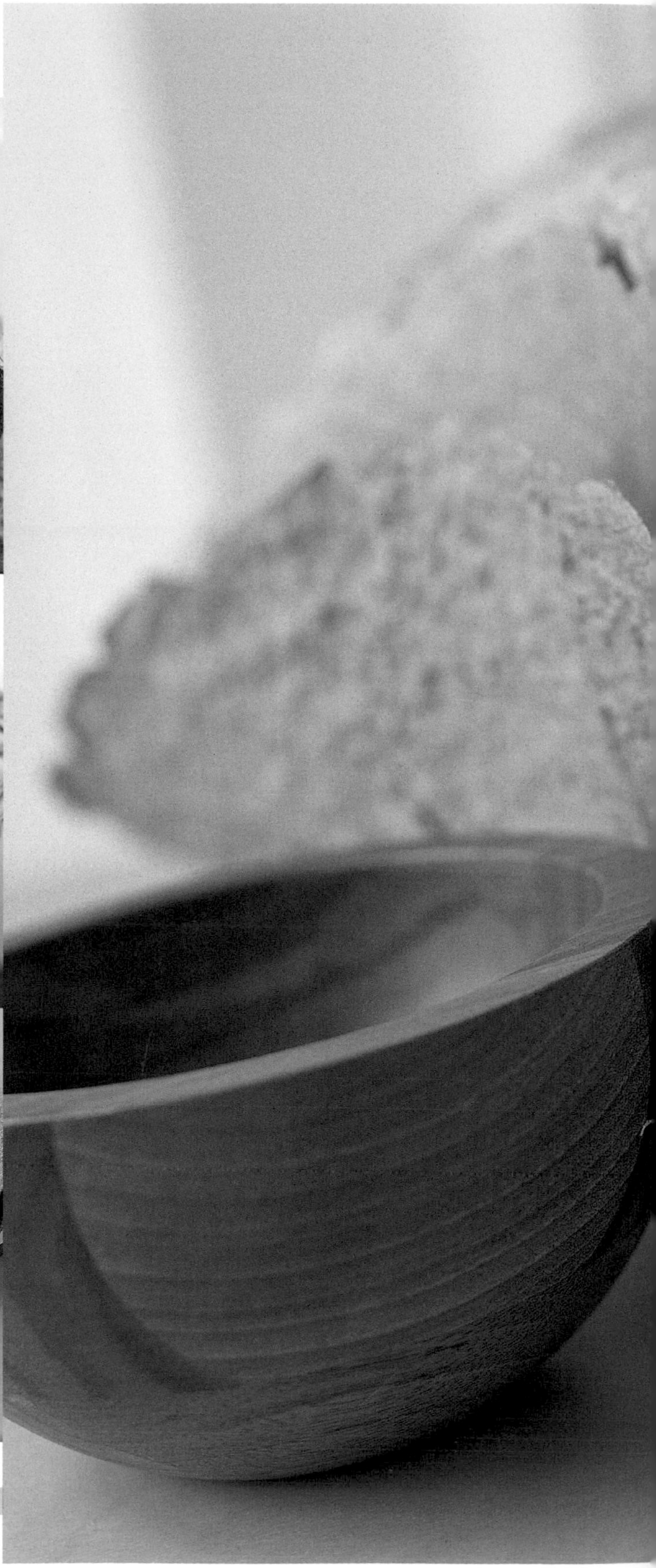

►
Soft, velvety textures on the back of living room chairs have *yin* qualities and are very tactile to touch.

Textures

Decorating the living room with various colors and textures creates an interesting place to relax, which is not only pleasing to look at, but which is also a space with sensual appeal.

The living room has a mixture of materials and surfaces, but it is our sense of touch that allows us to differentiate whether they are soft or hard, hot or cold, rough or smooth.

The surfaces of materials in the living room can also have an effect on the way *ch'i* flows and meanders through the room. Objects with a soft or rough texture, such as a pile of cushions or a throw, for example, have *yin* qualities, while hard, shiny objects such as a vase, a ceramic statue, a polished marble floor, or a mirror have very *yang* characteristics.

◄
The harder, more *yang* texture of this carefully turned wooden bowl, contrasts with the soft texture of fabrics.

▲
Brocade cushions, placed on sofas, bring a feeling of luxury and opulence to a living area.

The dining room

▲ Candles relate to the Fire Element and bring in some positive *yang* energy, which is always a must in the dining room.

▲ A round table is one of the best for dining. The round shape relates to the Metal Element so is associated with Wealth.

The dining room is pivotal to the harmony of the family or people within a household. It is a place that needs a good atmosphere for everyone to relax in, have good conversations, entertain, and to share good food together. The Chinese believe that eating feeds the spirit as well as the physical body, so the wellbeing of the diners is paramount. They believe that eating is a very social occasion and food plays a very important part in their culture. It is important that the family should eat at least one meal a day together to create harmony and balance in the home.

The room should not be a cramped, dark area which is cluttered with too much furniture. Ideally it should be square or rectangular in shape, have a round dining table (see Style File) and comfortable chairs, a sideboard, a mirror reflecting the abundance of the table, and not much else. An auspiciously oriented dining area with good lighting, bright colors and the right furniture is wealth enhancing as well as a center for perfect family bonding.

▲
A dining table that is full of food and drink is believed to enhance the prosperity and status of the family.

The best place to dine

The best location for the room where we regularly eat is toward the center of the home between the living room and the kitchen, making it the heart of the household. This will help to create greater harmony and understanding between parents and children. It should not be in direct view or have a line of sight to the front door. A dining area placed directly underneath a toilet on the floor above is not a good idea, as this "wet room" can suppress the good luck in the dining room.

If you live in an apartment, try to see the layout of the apartment above, to avoid placing your dining area directly under a toilet or kitchen. A rectangular or square room is thought to be the most auspicious, and also the easiest to decorate. If you are not able to have a separate dining room, create a special eating area, possible screened off from your living room.

A bright decor

The energy of the home is fuelled through all the food that is served, so the dining room is closely connected with the status and prosperity of the family. It is a room that will benefit from an abundance of *yang* energy to enhance this aspect of feng shui. This can be done with lights—especially crystal chandeliers—and candles, which bring in warmth and evoke the

The ideal dining room

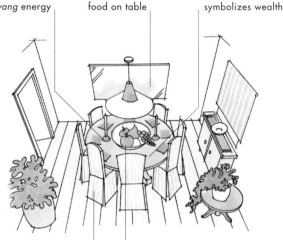

Candles for positive, intimate *yang* energy

Large mirror to symbolically double food on table

Circular table links to the Metal Element and symbolizes wealth

High-backed dining chairs give support: eight or six chairs are auspicious

Fruit on table is linked to abundance

▲ Setting a dining table attractively will help all the diners to enjoy the meal.

◄ Ideally the dining room should only contain a dining table, chairs, and sideboard to keep the focus on the food. The table will benefit from being well lit with a pendant light and candles to bring in *yang* energy and the warmth of the Fire Element.

► With regular family meals, try to orientate the seating so that everybody sits facing one of their Best Directions.

Fire Element. It can also be livened up by music and a pleasant, appealing decor using bright colors. Plants can encourage more *yang* energy and they also represent the growth of the family's good fortune.

Lucky seating

Check the number of place settings at the dining table as this will affect the luck of people living in your home. Ideally six, eight, or even nine are considered to be lucky—because odd numbers are *yang*. Of course, since household numbers tend to be fixed then your number of place settings cannot be altered daily. However, when you invite some guests to dinner, try to keep these auspicious numbers in mind.

Mirror placement

Mirrors are very powerful objects and by placing one strategically in the dining area so that it reflects the food on the table, you can symbolize the doubling of the family's wealth. This is the only place in the house where a mirror should reflect food. Never place a mirror near a stove or oven so that it reflects the food being cooked, as this is thought to increase the possibility of disaster such as accidents or a kitchen fire.

Auspicious symbols

You can enhance your feng shui luck in the dining room by using various lucky symbols. It is very auspicious to display the Chinese "Three Luck Gods" known as *Fuk, Luk,* and *Sau* as they represent wealth, health and longevity.

THE DINING ROOM | tips

○ Soften negative *ch'i* that emanates from sharp corners with plants or furniture.
○ Do not sit directly under a single large ceiling beam. If unavoidable, suspend two identical bamboo flutes on red strings on the beam, slanting them at 45° toward each other at the top, with the mouthpieces at the bottom end. This will help raise the beam's energy, reducing its negative vibrations.
○ Uplighters can also be installed and directed toward any offending beams to reduce negativity.
○ Every family member should try to orientate their dining seat to face one of their personal auspicious Directions based on their *kua* number (see pages 76–77).
○ Place paintings of fruits and food on the dining room wall to enhance Prosperity Luck.
○ Fruits such as oranges represent wealth as the word for "oranges" puns with the word for "gold" in some Chinese dialects.
○ Pictures representing longevity such as cranes, bamboo, or deer are also lucky symbols to boost the health of the diners.

▲
Round dining tables are considered auspicious in feng shui. They also have the added **advantage of having no sharp angles which could send cutting *ch'i* at the diners.**

style file

Tables

Sitting down to enjoy good food with family or friends in a congenial setting is one of life's most enjoyable experiences. In feng shui the table is the most important piece of furniture to get right in the dining room.

The best shape of dining table is round or oval. This is because it has no right angles or 'missing areas'. An octagonal table, not very common in the West, is also favored because the shape resembles the *pa kua*. Both types are supposed to bring favor to all who sit at them. Square and rectangular tables are also fine, but avoid seating guests at the corners where they could suffer from the bad *sha* off the angled points. It is also important to position the table beneath balanced lighting and in the center of the room for good ventilation.

Alternate men and women around the table for a good balance of *yin* and *yang*.

◄
The best shape for a dining table is round or oval. An even number of chairs is *yin*, an odd number *yang*.

▲
Even when a dining table is not in use you can make it look attractive by displaying fresh fruit and cut flowers.

◄ A formal table setting, as shown here, has very *yang* qualities. The table can be hardwood and strong, bold colors need to be used in the accessories. Candles add energy and also create a feeling of warmth and intimacy.

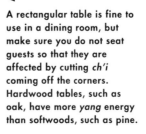

◄ A rectangular table is fine to use in a dining room, but make sure you do not seat guests so that they are affected by cutting *ch'i* coming off the corners. Hardwood tables, such as oak, have more *yang* energy than softwoods, such as pine.

▲ Choose your table accessories carefully. Glass and ceramic tableware is very *yang*, so balance these items with soft, flowing tablecloths and napkins in pastel colors.

▲
Especially when matched with a round table, modern curved chairs help to prevent any harmful cutting *ch'i*.

►
This modern beech chair with its metal legs would help to bring more *yang* energy into a dining room.

►
Yellow is a positive, *yang* color for the dining room, and the rounded, high back of this chair will give good, strong support at meal times.

Chairs

At a dinner party or a family meal it is important that the dining chairs are stylish but above all comfortable, so that they encourage people to linger and enjoy appetizing food, drink and convivial conversation.

Family members in particular should sit with their backs to a wall rather than a window when eating, as it will make them feel more secure. They should also move their chair so that it faces one of their auspicious Directions. Ideally, place chairs in even numbers round the dining table as it is more auspicious – six or eight is good for example, although odd numbers such as nine are also considered to be lucky.

High-backed dining chairs will also help to give support, while squarer chairs with straight lines and hard angles accelerate the movement of *ch'i* energy. Armless dining chairs with tall backs and upholstered seats are the perfect accompaniment to round dining tables as they create a balanced, harmonious environment.

Modern chairs with fluid, flowing shapes will prevent any *sha ch'i* coming off sharp angles and being directed at other diners. For more *yang* energy in your eating area, consider using metal or hardwood chairs; to bring in more *yin* energy buy some softwood styles instead.

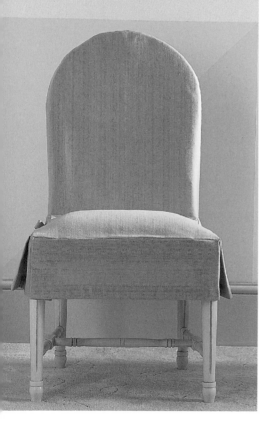

▼
The rounded arms of this wooden chair help *ch'i* to flow cleanly around the dining table.

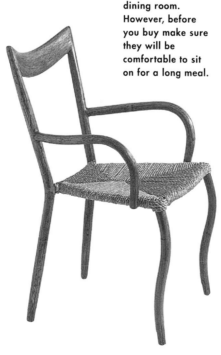

▲
Brightly colored, modern dining chairs in fluid shapes can be eyecatching in the dining room. However, before you buy make sure they will be comfortable to sit on for a long meal.

▲
Kitchen surfaces need to be kept uncluttered, so make as much use as possible of hanging units for kitchen utensils.

The
kitchen

Traditionally, the kitchen is the busy center of the home and, despite the increasing sophistication of our lives, it remains the focus of many domestic activities. Used primarily to prepare and cook food, it is also a place where friends pop round for a chat, and where the family may sit down to enjoy an informal meal together. In feng shui, the kitchen is associated with the nourishment and therefore the health of the family, so it should be arranged correctly as it is considered to be one of the most important rooms in the home.

However, the incompatible Elements of Fire and Water are in close proximity in the kitchen in appliances such as the oven, fridge, deep freeze, dishwasher and washing machine, so care must be taken with how their position so that they do not oppose each other. Surfaces need to be clean and free of clutter, so allow for adequate accessories and storage units (see style files). Use some *yang* textures, such as ceramic tiles, in inspiring colors, and create an inviting, nurturing environment.

◄
The kitchen is often
a good place for
all the family to
eat casual meals.
The informality and
warmth of the
room encourages
relaxed
conversation.

▲
Always make sure
in your kitchen that
your stove is not
next to or facing
your fridge or
freezer as the
Elements of these
appliances clash.

► If your kitchen is situated in the East of your home having wooden units will help to boost this beneficial Element.

The ideal kitchen

Sink positioned away from the stove

Good lighting is very important in the kitchen

Surfaces are kept uncluttered to aid flow of *ch'i*

A circular island unit lets the cook chat while preparing food

Healthy plants boost *ch'i* energy

▲ Ideally, a kitchen should be located in the East or Southeast of the home. As all the family's food is prepared here *Ch'i* circulation is very important, so have plenty of storage units to house accessories and appliances keeping surfaces clean and clutter-free.

THE KITCHEN tips

○ Store root vegetables in wire trays or wicker baskets for maximum aeration.

○ Combine neatly-fitted cupboards and shelves with adequate hanging racks and containers to keep everything neat and tidy.

○ Do not put too many gadgets on the worktops as clutter interferes with the flow of *ch'i.*

○ Try to include kitchen cabinets and worktops that have rounded edges to avoid potential *sha ch'i* which can cause family unhappiness and ill health.

○ Plug a microwave, toaster or kettle into one of your good Directions (see pages 76–77).

○ Always store large, sharp kitchen knives in a drawer or knife block to avoid 'cutting' *ch'i.*

○ Do not hang up strings of garlic or onions in the kitchen as they attract too much *yin* energy. Instead store them in vegetable racks.

○ Keep the fridge and freezer well stocked to show that there is abundance in the home and that the family will never be short of food.

The social center

The kitchen is the place that nourishes all the occupants of the home and in feng shui terms it is believed to reflect the fortunes of the family since the quality of the food is thought to show the wealth of the family. It is also important to have free-flowing *ch'i*, good positioning of appliances, and uncluttered surfaces. The doorway should be free of blockages, and any jutting corners which could generate 'cutting' *ch'i* should be eliminated.

The kitchen, as the heart of the home, should be shielded from the front door so that it is not immediately visible when entering the house. If this is not possible, at least keep the kitchen door closed at all times. Worktops should be positioned in such a way that you do not have your back to the door too much when preparing or cooking food, as this can create feelings of unease and insecurity.

Good location

The best location in your home for your kitchen is in your *tien yi* (health) direction determined from your *kua* number (see pages 76–77). If your kitchen is not situated here, try at least to organize the stove and oven 'fire mouth' – now seen as the source of gas or electricity for the appliances – points in this direction. The importance of these cooking appliances in feng shui is that they are the source of nourishment for the family, and represent both health and wealth.

Other suitable places for the kitchen are the East and Southeast of your home as the Wood Element in these directions is compatible with both Fire and Water. In the Element Productive Cycle of feng shui, Wood feeds Fire and is nourished by Water.

Alternatively, you can enhance the Wood Element by using the color green which symbolizes it, or display some wooden accessories to encourage some more Wood energy into the kitchen.

Clashing of the Elements

The kitchen always contains many appliances and many of these are associated with one or other of the Five Elements (see pages 30–41). The oven and stove are associated with the Fire Element and are very important. They should not be face either the front or back doors of the home as valuable *ch'i* can be lost. Siting them next to, or directly opposite, the fridge, deep freeze, sink or dishwasher is not auspicious as all these appliances are associated with the Water Element. In the Destructive Cycle of feng shui, Water destroys Fire, therefore the confrontation between these two Elements may lead to quarrels and misunderstandings in the household.

▼
A stove like this which is constantly hot serves the dual purpose in a kitchen of cooking the family's food and also giving out a pleasant warmth.

Accessories

The kitchen is the focus of many domestic activities for all family members so different accessories are needed to assist with food preparation, cooking and eating. To keep *ch'i* flowing freely kitchen surfaces should be kept as uncluttered as possible, so you need to buy a few carefully chosen accessories to hold all the relevant gadgets that you regularly use for cooking.

Ceramic, terracotta or wooden containers look stunning on work surfaces and can be used to hold a variety of cooking utensils. Wall racks with smooth, curved lines can hold wine glasses or mugs and, because they have no sharp edges, you will be protected from any cutting *ch'i* coming at you while you are cooking.

Metallic toasters and kettles can boost the *yang* element of the kitchen, but with sharp metal items such as knives, rather than having them on a wall rack, store them away in a cutlery drawer in a unit or hide their sharp, unsightly edges in a knife block to avoid any *sha ch'i*.

▼
A variety of wooden and metallic hanging racks are available for kitchen utensils so that you keep them off the work surface. However, be careful of racks that hang above central units as they can create a feeling of pressure for the cook working underneath them.

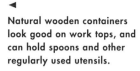

◄ Natural wooden containers look good on work tops, and can hold spoons and other regularly used utensils.

► This curved cutlery unit is ideal in a modern kitchen, and because of its shape there is no threat of *sha ch'i*.

▲ You can also store glasses on hanging units, such as this wave-shaped one.

▼ Metal electrical items add a *yang* quality to the kitchen area.

▲ Glass bowls are more *yang* accessories. Fill them with seasonal fruit or vegetables or use them for salad on the dinner table.

style file

▶

A stone floor can be rather cold underfoot in a kitchen, but it will last a long time and will keep *ch'i* flowing freely.

▲

This linoleum flooring feels warm underfoot, is very hardwearing and is a practical addition to a kitchen as it is so easy to clean.

◀

Wooden flooring is easy to clean and has a warmth and rich texture. However, in this kitchen the flow of *ch'i* may be a bit slow as there are also wooden units.

◄

Stone flooring is very hardwearing in a kitchen and can complement the more *ying* energies coming from wooden kitchen units.

Flooring

Floors form a large surface in any room, and in a hardworking room such as a kitchen deciding on the right type of flooring is a difficult decision. The ideal situation is to reach a perfect balance of *yin* and *yang*, incorporating both hard and soft surfaces in the room.

The flow of *ch'i* energy throughout your home can be influenced by the flooring material and different materials have different effects. Wooden flooring is warm and rich in texture, is easy to clean, and doesn't affect the flow of *ch'i*. Harder materials, such as marble, granite, slate or stone are very *yang* and so they speed up the flow of *ch'i* across their surfaces.

Conversely, softer *yin* surfaces, such as seagrass, sisal and cork tiles will slow down the movement of *ch'i*. So, when you're planning your kitchen flooring think about how it will balance with your units. If your units are all wood, for example, a more *yang* flooring such as stone or granite will complement and balance them.

However, if you have large expanses of marble or granite work surfaces, adding sisal flooring or coir matting will add the necessary *yin* energy to create kitchen harmony.

style file

◄ Open shelving displaying items such as these stainless steel canisters and saucepans can be an eye-catching feature of a kitchen.

◄ Here, hanging hooks have been placed behind the stove to allow for more utensil hanging space.

▲ Displaying different shapes and styles of crockery in glass-fronted cupboards can add a pleasing effect to a kitchen.

Storage

The kitchen is a very important place in feng shui because it's the room that provides the family's main source of nourishment. Full refrigerators, freezers and store cupboards symbolize the family's wealth, and maintaining a good stock of provisions indicates that the family will always stay healthy and happy. However, it is not a good idea to keep food beyond its sell-by date as this will create negative energies, so check through your cupboards regularly and throw away any products that have gone stale.

Kitchen surfaces should also look streamlined and open, since leaving too many items on top of the work surfaces will slow down the flow of *ch'i*. Try to keep produce, china, utensils and cutlery out of the way by storing them in kitchen cabinets, or hanging them from racks. Fruit or vegetables piled in hanging baskets can look very appealing and the effect of fresh produce spilling over creates a feeling of abundance. Storage jars, utensils and other accessories can look great sitting on open shelves but make sure you place them close to the sharp edges to prevent any *sha ch'i*.

▲
You can choose whether to use free-standing or fitted cabinets in the kitchen, but always plan enough space for the accessories you'll buy in **the future. Using a warm orange color on the walls and cabinets can really help lift the energy, giving the whole kitchen a positive boost.**

The
bathroom

Whether you're seeking a quick energizing shower, or a long relaxing soak in the bath, modern bathrooms are havens designed to help you unwind from the hectic pressures of everyday life. Relaxing bath oils, scented soaps and candles – for a bit of Fire energy – can all add to the atmosphere (see style files).

To create the ideal feng shui bathroom, location, colors, materials and textures must all be given consideration. One of the most satisfying rooms to decorate, because of its relatively small size, a bathroom gives you the opportunity to use some different materials and schemes that might seem too indulgent for other parts of the house.

More often than not, most of us have little choice about the positions of our bathrooms – but we can take steps to benefit from good locations, as well as alleviate other less fortunate ones. The bathroom is one of the most draining, *yin* areas in the home because of the amount of water that is used there, so ensure it is well ventilated to create an airy ambience, and prevent any damp or stagnant energy gathering there.

▲
Biscuit tones and soft colors such as this yellow are auspicious in a bathroom.

◄
Stylish, chrome taps look great in a modern bathroom. They are very *yang* and will help to balance the existing *yin* energy.

►
A bathroom is a place where we can indulge our design fantasies – after all, it is a place where we spend a lot of time pampering ourselves.

A haven of calm

Ideally, bathrooms should be located along the sides of your home. The toilet itself should be hidden from view, or as far away from the main door as possible, to minimize the draining of *ch'i* energy from the rest of your home. A simple cure for a badly located toilet is to ensure the lid is kept shut and keep the bathroom door closed at all times. An outward-facing, full-length mirror on the door also helps.

Plant power

Houses today have more bathrooms than ever before. In feng shui terms water is associated with Wealth and the number of bathrooms, toilets and the condition of the plumbing in a home can affect its occupants' financial condition. An inauspicious configuration of these 'wet rooms' can drain the positive energy flowing around a home, and a bathroom sited in the Southeast may actively flush away the Wealth luck of a household. Plants will help mitigate this situation, as Wood 'feeds' on Water in the Element Productive Cycle.

The best colors

The best choice of bathroom colors would be pastel shades – pinks, light greens and blues as well as peach. Alternative colors are creams, biscuit tones and other neutral shades. Black and white are also good, particularly if accentuated with some bold splashes

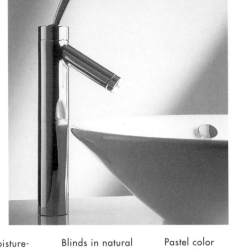

A vast array of tap fittings are now available, allowing you to create whatever style of room you want.

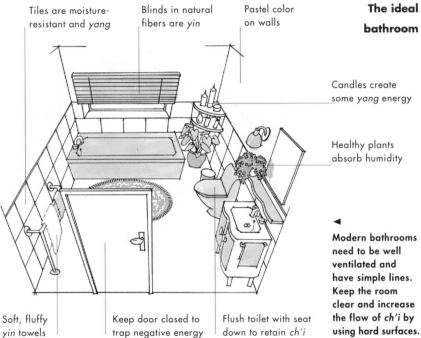

The ideal bathroom

Tiles are moisture-resistant and *yang*

Blinds in natural fibers are *yin*

Pastel color on walls

Candles create some *yang* energy

Healthy plants absorb humidity

Soft, fluffy *yin* towels

Keep door closed to trap negative energy

Flush toilet with seat down to retain *ch'i*

Modern bathrooms need to be well ventilated and have simple lines. Keep the room clear and increase the flow of *ch'i* by using hard surfaces.

▲

This unusual shower unit and bath area contains chrome, glass and ceramic tiling which all very *yang*.

of color provided by interesting accessories and towels.

Clutter free

Minimum clutter is essential and the most desirable bathrooms are those that have simple, clean lines, and which are airy. Obviously, surfaces need to be water resistant and easy to clean, and generally hard surfaces, such as wood, marble, tile or vinyl are preferable to soft rugs and carpets. Marble, granite and other hard, smooth surfaces, for example, speed up the flow of *ch'i* energy, especially if they are shiny and reflective. They help create a more exciting environment, and one that helps avoid stagnation.

Good lighting

Bright lights are essential in the bathroom to stimulate *ch'i* energy. Halogen downlighters recessed in the

◄

The dramatic blue decor of this bathroom really makes the white ceramic basin and bath stand out.

THE BATHROOM tips

○ If your bathroom has no windows, create the illusion of space by hanging a mirror on the wall.

○ Good ventilation is advisable in the bathroom to help dispel humidity.

○ Plenty of plants absorb humidity and make the room feel fresh and alive, minimizing the risk of any *ch'i* energy stagnating in the corners.

○ If the bathroom door opens directly onto another room, keep it shut at all times to prevent negative energy spreading through the rest of your home.

○ Keep bathroom surfaces as uncluttered as possible and use minimal furniture as too many objects create a damp, stagnant atmosphere.

○ Ensuite bathrooms are not favored in feng shui because of their proximity to the bedroom. If you have one, always keep the door closed.

○ Keep the toilet seat down when you are flushing it to reduce negativity, as you are believed to be flushing away *ch'i* and the family's finances, as water is also linked with money.

ceiling are especially effective with some additional task lighting for make-up and shaving. Curtains and blinds made of natural fibers will contrast with the more *yang* flooring.

Bathrooms today are all about relaxation and escapism. Whether you prefer contemporary tiles and gleaming marble, or more traditional fixtures and fittings, surround yourself with materials and textures that make your bathroom your own personal haven of privacy and contemplation.

Aromas

Although an essential place for everyone to shower or bathe, the bathroom is unfortunately also considered the least auspicious room by feng shui masters because of the stagnant energy it contains and the large amount of water it drains – and water is linked with money.

However, this doesn't mean that it should not be a pleasant, inviting room, a place to retreat to for some well-deserved cosseting after a hard day's work. Once you get the layout and color scheme right you can concentrate on creating the right type of atmosphere.

To help calm you down, burn some relaxing incense or aromatherapy oil, such as lavender, in an oil burner. As the bathroom is very *yin*, because of its water-draining qualities, light a variety of candles, both scented and plain, to make it more *yang* and positive. Use sensuous, tactile soaps, fragrant shower gels, luxurious bath oils or foams to appeal to your senses and make your bathing experience a very special one.

 Keep a variety of candles in the bathroom and light them when bathing to give off some positive *yang* energy.

▼ Fragrant bath balls slowly dissolve in the water to give off delicious, appealing scents.

◄ Soothe the senses in the bathroom by burning aromatherapy oils. Geranium and lavender oil are particularly calming.

◄ Choose soaps for the bathroom that appeal to all the senses. They need to look attractive, smell pleasant and should also feel good to the touch.

▲ Incense sticks, scented with oils such as sandalwood or lemon grass, are another good way of bringing about a relaxed bathroom environment. Light one a few moments before you bathe.

▲ Scented stones can be placed around the bath and basin in the bathroom to add pleasant aromatic scents and some more *yang* energy.

style file

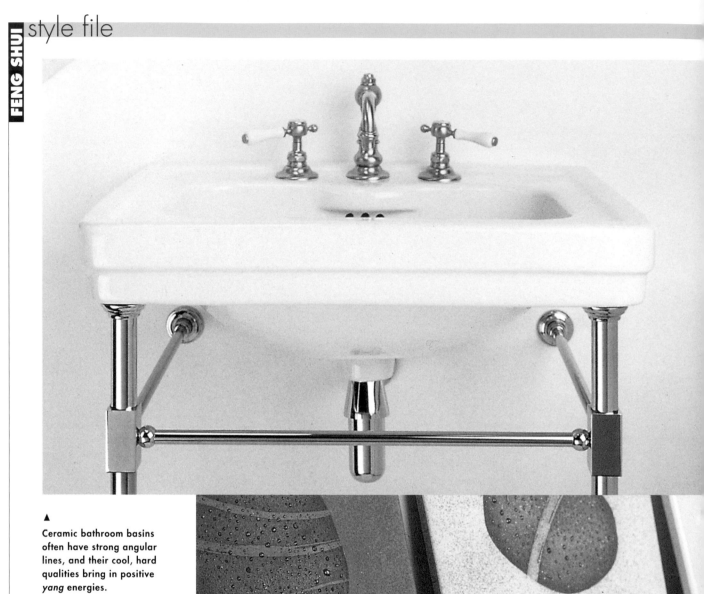

▲

Ceramic bathroom basins often have strong angular lines, and their cool, hard qualities bring in positive *yang* energies.

▶

Tiles can be a large feature of a bathroom and add to its overall appeal. Their hard, shiny surfaces help the room's positivity. When choosing tiles try to select the patterns and shapes that will enhance the room's Element.

Textures

As with every other room in the house, hard and soft surfaces and textures need to be harmonized in the bathroom. As there is a tendency for stagnant energy to gather here it is better to have more *yang* materials to offset this. Ceramic bathroom suites are very *yang* as are wall and floor tiles. Chrome taps and accessories also have *yang* qualities.

They add to the style of a bathroom and because of their reflective surfaces help to speed up the flow of *ch'i*. Mirrors reflect light bringing in positive energy and expanding the space in a small bathroom. Wood accessories add a welcome warmth, while the presence of tactile, fluffy towels bath robes and bathroom mats brings in balancing *yin* energies.

▲
The smooth, sleek lines of chrome accessories contrast well with white bathroom suites, and they also help to lift the energy.

◄
Natural wood units exude warmth and appeal in the bathroom. They can be used to house soft towels, bath sets and other bathroom accessories.

The
bedroom

Your bedroom is one of the most important rooms in the house because it is the place you can lie down and relax after a hard day's work at the office, or looking after children at home. It is also where you get restorative sleep, which is essential for good health and communication with your family. A calm, pleasant *yin* environment with restful colors is ideal with soft flowing fabrics and a comfortable, but supportive bed. Furniture and clutter should be kept to a minimum so that *ch'i* can gently meander around the room and encourage restful sleep.

It is also an intimate room where you sleep and make love with your partner, so good feng shui is essential to nurture you and a loving relationship. Positioning the bed correctly, keeping electrical equipment to a minimum, and removing anything to do with work can all help to achieve the right feeling. Burning essential oils, such as geranium or lavender, before you sleep can also create the relaxing, inviting atmosphere that you need.

▲
A bedroom needs to be a restful, calm environment with soothing colors and soft, tactile fabrics.

►
Natural fabrics enhance the relaxing atmosphere of the bedroom and are also gentle on the eye.

A tranquil sanctuary

When the bedroom is laid out auspiciously it brings harmony to all the family who will then be more likely to enjoy good health, a successful relationship or marital bliss. The ambience in this room must have predominantly more *yin* energy to make it restful and to bring about sound sleep, with no restless or negative energies in the room.

The bedroom is an area that needs to be clean and clear of the clutter which can cause the flow of energy to stagnate. Soft, flowing fabrics and natural cotton or linen duvets can add to the desired *yin* and overall relaxing effect.

Black is not a good color for the bedroom as it is too *yin* while bright red which is too *yang* – as elsewhere in the home always try to keep a good balance of energies. Pastel shades can be good but blue is the best color to use in bedrooms – it is *yin* which brings calm and restfulness to the room.

The shape of the room

The best bedroom have a regular shape with no missing areas of the *pa kua*. For example, an L-shaped room, created by an en-suite bathroom, will present problems as it has a missing corner which upsets the energy flow in the room. Also, 'poison arrows' could come off the sharp corner formed by the walls and disturb sleep if they point towards the bed. The ideal shape for a bedroom is a rectangle or square.

Positioning the bed

As with the room, the bed needs to be regular in shape, and water or circular beds are not recommended. Water beds especially disturb the good feng shui of a bedroom. Natural, wooden beds are best. Take care with iron beds as they can conduct electricity from appliances or radiators.

Double beds are the most auspicious for relationships – two separate beds or one bed with two single mattresses suggests an unstable relationship and in time may lead to upset or separation.

Never place the bed under a window as this symbolizes lack of support. Also, the end of the bed should not face the bedroom door as this is called the 'death position' and needs to be avoided. Choose a bed with a sturdy headboard and place it against a solid wall for good support. However, don't let it share a wall with an en-suite toilet as it may take on that room's negative energies.

Ideally, the bedhead should point in the direction of your third best position or *nien yen* for family relationship and harmony. To find out your *nien yen* position, you need to calculate your *kua* number based on your date of birth (see pages 76–77). This will then give you the four auspicious directions in which you can orientate your bed and the four inauspicious ones to avoid.

Overhead cupboards

Cupboards and wardrobes that are suspended over the head of a bed create a similar harmful effect to beams. This is a popular wardrobe design as it creates extra storage space, but negative *ch'i* will flow downwards from the suspended cupboard towards the people lying in bed underneath. This, in turn, may cause either headaches or even disturbed sleep.

Try to remove the suspended section completely. Alternatively, if space permits, pull the bed out of reach of the suspended wardrobe and place a set of cabinets behind to fill in the empty space that is left. If this isn't possible, hang two bamboo flutes from the cupboard to raise its energy as if it was a beam.

Another approach is to design a tenting feature of thick fabric to cover the bottom of the suspended cupboard like a canopy. This creates a romantic feature in the bedroom, while at the same time it protects the occupants from the adverse effects of the overhead negative energy.

Open shelves

Generally in feng shui open shelves are not recommended anywhere in

◄

Natural wooden beds are best for undisturbed sleep as they don't affect the energy of the room. If you have a shelf behind your bed, as shown here, try to keep it uncluttered or you may feel the burden of objects pressing down on you when sleeping.

▲

Soft, inviting candlelight gives an extra warmth to the bedroom. It can also lift the energy slightly, adding to the romantic, loving environment.

◄ As the bedroom is supposed to be a very calm place, remove electrical equipment as items have too much *yang* energy and can cause infidelity. If you can't bear to get rid of the television, cover the screen at night.

The ideal bedroom

Bedside lamps create *yin* energy and intimacy.

Bedroom mirrors must not reflect bed.

Cover square units with cloths to prevent *sha ch'i*

Silk flowers – real flowers are too *yang*

► A bedroom needs to be calm and restful. Have no electical equipment and use a battery alarm clock.

Bed diagonally opposite door.

Wood-framed bed with supportive headboard

Round-edged furniture to avoid *sha ch'i*

the home as poison arrows can emanate from their blade-like edges. It is especially harmful in the bedroom to sleep opposite a row of open shelves as the continued exposure to this harmful energy while sleeping can cause sickness.

To counteract this the ideal situation is to convert the shelves into cupboards by adding some doors to create small wardrobes. Alternatively, you can pack the shelves tightly and uniformly with books so that you reduce the overall effect of the poison arrows.

▲
Plan your furniture for the bedroom carefully, keep it minimal, but maybe include a treasured chair and an inspirational painting or statue.

◄
If you prefer to sleep in an iron bed, soften the head board with cushions. Also, keep it away from radiators as it may conduct electricity from them.

THE BEDROOM tips

❍ To boost romance for both couples and single people, display a pair of mandarin ducks in the Southwest of the bedroom or near the bed.

❍ You can also display the 'double happiness' symbol – Chinese calligraphy for happiness and love. They are normally gold on red card – a good luck color.

❍ Avoid plants and flowers in the bedroom as they produce excessive *yang* energy. They can also cause acrimonious feelings and even unfaithfulness between a couple.

❍ Avoid water features, aquariums or paintings of water in the bedroom as it is believed that water indicates the probability of a robbery, burglary or a financial loss.

❍ Soften sharp corners from walls, wardrobes, or other furniture producing 'poison arrows' across the bed by hanging a lead-faceted crystal in front of it or softening with a cloth.

❍ Pendulum lights or ceiling fans should not be positioned directly over the bed as this will generate poison arrows and disturb sleep.

❍ The bedroom door should not align with the toilet door nor face another door or staircase in the corridor or landing. If the bed lies between the toilet door and the bedroom door, it may cause ill fortune. Placing a screen in front of the en-suite bathroom door will shield off any negative energy.

❍ Avoid sleeping under a beam. If you have to, hang two bamboo flutes with the mouthpieces at the bottom (see *Dining Room Tips*, page 103)

❍ Do not allow a mirror or TV to reflect the bed as it will cause disturbed sleep, may result in bad health, strained relationships, or it may bring a third party into the relationship. If they cannot be moved, cover at night.

Lighting

Bedrooms are one of our most important relaxation zones where we recover from the stresses of the day and get some regenerative sleep, and it is here that our spirit rests. They are very *yin* places, so the lighting needs to have a good ambience, and be soft and soothing to enhance a feeling of calm. Do not use harsh or bright lights over the bed as they can upset the balance of the room and can sometimes bring problems with eyesight.

Dimmer switches help to create the right level of light, and work well with pendant shades in pleasing, rounded shapes in sensuous materials such as silk or muslin. Big shades with sharp, pointed edges should be avoided as they can send cutting *ch'i* across the bed and, in time, cause illness for the occupants.

Bedside lamps with rounded shades and bases placed near the bed can give the task lighting needed for late-night reading. Scented candles of different shapes and sizes have a warm, inviting perfume and glow – adding to the romance of the bedroom, particularly if they are placed in the Relationships area in Southwest – but remember that they should never be left unattended.

▲
Modern or more traditional styles of lamps can be used to suit the bedroom decoration.

◀
Patterned lampshades can be chosen to blend in with the colors that relate to the bed's position and Element.

► Modern, adjustable lamps suit bedtime reading, just make sure that the light is not too harsh.

▼ Bedroom lighting needs to be more *yin* than usual, so use bedside lamps with shades that give a soft glow.

▼ Light some scented or plain candles to give a warm, inviting aroma and soft glow in the bedroom.

Bed linen

The type of bed linen that you use can add to its warmth, color and romance. As the bedroom is a very *yin* environment the fabrics will support this. Natural fibers are best, so buy your sheets, pillow cases, duvets, valances and bed hangings in pure cotton, linen or sensuous silk.

Choose fabrics that feel good and soft to the touch. As you spend a third of your life asleep in your bed, being comfortable is vital.

If you decide to hang a canopy above your bed, select fabrics that drape gracefully in soft folds. Muslin and silk are both ideal as they allow the *ch'i* energy to flow gently around the bed.

When deciding on colors and patterns for your bed linen, match them to the corner of the room where the bed is positioned. So, for example, if your bed is in the East, shades of green would be appropriate, especially if combined with a pattern which incorporates squares as these both support the Earth energy.

Use a plain-colored bedspread if you are unsure whether a design may prove harmful. Avoid using duvets or pillow cases that have very abstract prints or triangular or pointed patterns as these are linked to the Fire Element and would create too much *yang* energy in what is supposed to be the most peaceful room in the house.

► You can choose to boost the color of your bed's Element on the fabric that you use for the padded headboard.

◄ Here, pleasing neutral colors have been used for the bed fabrics. Blue has been brought in on the headboard to support the bed's northerly position.

▲
Bed hangings in
soft, silky fabrics
look rich and very
welcoming. They
also create gentle
flowing folds that
encourage *ch'i*
energy to
meander slowly
around them.

▼
White bed linen
always looks fresh
and appealing. If
the bed is in the
West of the
bedroom it will
also enhance the
Metal Element.

The
children's
bedroom

▲
If the bedroom is large enough, include a rocking horse as it is a perennial favorite with all children.

►
As well as being a place to sleep, a child's bedroom is also a playroom, so allow enough space for them to store all their favorite toys.

▼
A drawing and painting table can keep children occupied for hours. As it is a creative area you can use strong, bold colors.

Children need constant care and support. They like to feel safe and secure but they also need their own space and privacy. The bedroom is the most important room in their world. It is their special haven where they can play and have fun during the day, but it is also a place for them to be at peace and to sleep soundly at night.

However, if the feng shui of your child or children's bedroom is wrong – if, for example, they are sleeping under a badly sloping roof or on the bottom of bunk beds – it can have a detrimental effect on the entire family. Unless you are lucky enough to have a separate playroom, a young child's bedroom needs to have plenty of room to allow for both sleeping, having friends round, and a variety of playing activities.

By painting the room a restful color, using the right fabrics and textures, and keeping the room free of mess with bright storage accessories you can create a calm but inspiring place for your child or children.

Room planning

A well-organized and clutter-free space will encourage beneficial, positive *ch'i* energy into kids' rooms. Children are notoriously messy – but an untidy room can make it difficult for them to think and act clearly, because clutter hampers the flow of *ch'i*. Try to allow adequate storage (see pages 140–141) and encourage children to put their toys away at night before they go to bed: choose easy-to-reach floor boxes and toy chests but steer clear of heavy lids that could trap little fingers.

Sweet dreams

If a child is not sleeping well, check his or her sleeping direction. Try to make sure they are sleeping with their head pointed towards either their *sheng ch'i* or *nien yen* direction, determined from their *kua* number (see pages 56–57). Avoid positioning the bedhead where it has anything hanging over it, such as a shelf or cupboard, a beam, or a sloping ceiling. These all create downward energy pressure on the child, causing very restless sleep.

Storing anything underneath the bed may also hamper sleep. Avoid placing the bedhead below a window, as this doesn't give the support that a wall does and encourages a flow of active *ch'i* energy which will again prevent a good night's sleep.

Ideally, furniture should be made of natural materials with rounded edges, avoiding sharp corners which create harmful, cutting *sha ch'i*. Curved, rounded furniture not only promotes the flow of *ch'i* in a room, but also reduces the risk of nasty accidents.

Color care

When decorating the bedroom, take into account both your child's present age and their changing character as they grow up. Bright colors look good but may over-stimulate very active children. Similarly, busily patterned wallpaper and fabrics and primary colors such as red, which is very *yang*, should be avoided and replaced with more subtle shades, particularly if you have an over-active child.

Decorate walls with pictures drawn by your children or toys they have made themselves – a seashell mobile, for example, can be a visual record of a holiday by the sea.

Changing needs

As children grow up, the bedroom develops from nursery and play area to teenager's den. Priorities change too, and instead of a clear floor space for all their toys, they are likely to need more work space for hobbies, homework and a computer.

Encourage reading by positioning lamps next to beds and enhance a desire for knowledge by hanging a crystal in the Northeast of the room, the knowledge and education sector. Enhancing the West sector of the *pa kua* – children's luck – affects the

◄
Young babies love these bright animal mats to play on. Choose one which has bright, primary colors as they always find these very appealing.

►
Use hanging bags to store any extra toys and games.

THE CHILDREN'S BEDROOM tips

○ A mobile is relaxing for young children, but do not hang it directly over the bed.

○ If your child's bedroom door faces a bathroom or staircase it can make them rebellious and lacking in motivation, so hang a small wind chime above the door.

○ A solid, well-attached, headboard, provides children with support and a sense of security.

○ Do not use bunk beds as they can make the child on the bottom feel he or she is being compressed.

○ Screen off a computer from the bed, and switch it off at night to reduce electromagnetic stress.

○ If a TV is in the room, make sure it does not face the bed as it is bad feng shui to reflect the child when sleeping. If it cannot be moved, cover it with a cloth at night.

○ Place a clear quartz or amethyst crystal on study desks to boost education luck.

▲
When space is tight, a bed which has drawers built in underneath can prove very useful for storing clothes.

Colorful bed linen and wall hangings make the room bright and inviting – just right for a lively, young child.

The ideal children's bedroom

Natural fabric blind

Inspiring fabric wallhanging to slow *ch'i* energy

Rounded play table to prevent *sha ch'i*

Colorful duvets

Durable wooden toys

Door to be kept closed at night to slow energy

Twin beds rather than bunk beds

Brightly colored storage units to keep toys off floor

overall health, behaviour and academic performance of your children and is well worth checking, particularly if a child seems unhappy.

By using these simple feng shui techniques, you can make your child's bedroom a harmonious living space.

▲
An overcrowded room affects how children function, so allow plenty of storage space. Decorate the room brightly, and use interesting bed linen, wall hangings and pictures.

style file

Storage

Kids always own a lot of toys and school equipment which often gets strewn around their bedroom, and the problem is doubled if two kids share a room. But an overcrowded bedroom will inhibit the flow of *ch'i* and adversely affect how the children think and act. Get your children to throw out old toys as these will hold them back, and encourage them to put their toys away at night to calm the room's energy.

▼

Coordinate a child's bedroom by using **bright fabrics to cover the furniture.**

◄

Fabric storage holders can hold small toys. Hang them on the back of doors or cupboards.

►

Wooden storage units have shelves to hold books, toys and boxes.

▼

You can mix and match hanging and fixed storage. Make sure toys are put away each night.

Plastic boxes which stack on top of each other are a good idea as they can hold many toys and be kept neatly at the sides of the room. But do not stack them too high or they could be oppressive, and choose appealing colors, such as pastels, that will not be overstimulating.

Wooden units with shallow drawers can hold all sorts of small toys. Keep them near the ground so that the children can put things away themselves. Natural woven or wicker baskets have more flexibility as they stretch, and can hold every sort of wooden toys as well as fluffy animals and dolls.

The
garden

Feng shui in our homes shows us how best to align ourselves in our environment. A true feng shui garden should follow nature's lead as much as possible with the primary aim of creating harmony and balance.

Planting trees or large shrubs will give the protection needed at the back of your garden, and you can create balance by mixing shapes and sizes of plants so that no one species overwhelms the others. Allowing paths to meander through the garden will echo the movement of *ch'i* energy. If they are straight, allow plants to grow over them so that the *ch'i* can circulate around them.

Water features and ponds are beautiful and relaxing at any time of the year – they also attract *ch'i* and symbolize prosperity. Extra *yang* energy can be encouraged with garden lights which will also light up any of the garden's dark corners.

▲
Paths should never be straight as *ch'i* energy would rush too quickly towards your home. Instead, let them curve through your garden, so that they encourage the energy to flow slowly and freely through the area.

►
Create havens in your garden where you and your family can relax while enjoying the sunshine and afternoon tea.

►►
Include small and tall shrubs and a mixture of different colored flowers to achieve a balance of *yin* and *yang*.

Garden planning

For centuries the garden has played a significant role as an adjunct to the home – a special place where the family can relax and entertain friends, and a sanctuary where plants and flowers can grow. The garden is a versatile space, a place that can be transformed easily to improve the feng shui and attract precious *ch'i* energy into our lives. In ancient China, gardens were designed to mirror nature's landscape and reap the benefits of feng shui for their owners. For example, rocks representing mountains were placed in skilfully cultivated gardens and beautiful ponds were constructed in the correct place to represent rivers and lakes.

A fertile garden

To make the perfect feng shui garden, grow a good mix of flowers, shrubs and trees that will delight the senses with fragrance or color in all four seasons. Ensure plants are lush, healthy and well-trimmed, and that the shapes balance each other to encourage good feng shui for your home and its occupants. Encourage Wealth, Luck, and Prosperity by growing healthy plants in the Southeast of the garden.

Strive to achieve a balance of *yin* and *yang* in the garden. The presence of soft *yin* foliage can be

balanced with the *yang* of natural stone and rock. Introduce stone ornaments and terracotta plant containers for a touch of Earth energy, particularly in the Southwest and Northeast. Stone, wood, and metal all have their place, and you will need to check your *pa kua* (see pages 26–29) to determine in which sector each should be placed.

Climbers

Most of us who live in towns and cities have garden walls and fences that are not of our own choosing. Don't despair: you can turn them to your own advantage by using them to support climbing plants and flowers. This not only adds color and height to a garden, but, with planning, these plants can soften any sharp edges or corners and reduce harmful, cutting *ch'i*.

◄ Use a variety of materials in a garden to bring about the effect you want. Gravel and brick are very *yang* and can help to mark out seating areas and garden borders.

► In a larger area grow a mixture of flowering and evergreen shrubs up pergolas to create a structural effect.

A rustic wooden bench looks perfect in a country garden, and if it is placed in the East it will help to boost the Wood Element.

THE GARDEN

tips

❍ Placing garden lights in the Southwest sector of your garden may bring significant gains to the marital and relationship spheres of your life.

❍ Plant strong, fast-growing shrubs or small trees to add support and protect the back of the garden.

❍ Always remember to remove any dried leaves and faded blooms from plants as these are dead items and create negative *ch'i*.

❍ Whether it's a garden pond, a fountain, or even a bird bath, a healthy water feature is an essential addition to a feng shui garden.

❍ Be careful, however, of too much water near your home, swimming pools are very *yin* and if the size is not planned carefully they can overwhelm you.

❍ Small courtyards or patios can benefit from climbing shrubs or plants to bring in extra *ch'i*.

❍ Never leave dead tree stumps, rotting plants or vegetation in the garden as they all create *sha ch'i*.

❍ Rocks can add some strong *yang* energy to contrast with the softer *yin* energy of plants.

A good area

Our homes are generally made of hard, straight lines, so contrast this by creating natural curves and softness with borders, lawns and trees to maintain a balance and encourage *ch'i* to flow in a slow, lazy fashion.

Creating paths that meander through the garden will also encourage *ch'i* energy to flow gently through the space. For a little indulgence, illuminate your garden with lights and lanterns that are specially designed for the outdoors.

style file

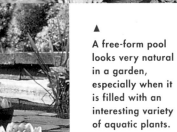

▲

Elaborate water
features can
become the main
focus of a garden,
but make sure its
size doesn't
overpower the rest
of the garden.

▲

A free-form pool
looks very natural
in a garden,
especially when it
is filled with an
interesting variety
of aquatic plants.

▶

Goldfish are
considered to be
very auspicious in
feng shui. Nine is
an excellent
number to keep
in a pond.

▼

An established pond
needs to be well
maintained as any
dead plants or
sickly fish can
create stagnant
ch'i energy.

▶

If you only have
room for a small
water feature,
ensuring that
water circulates
constantly will
make it as
advantageous as
a larger one.

▲
An elaborate garden water feature that cascades down over rocks will appeal to all.

►
Ponds can be an attractive sight in a garden, but placing them in the best feng shui location is essential.

Water

Trickling, gurgling, splashing or murmuring, water features in the garden are beautiful all year – a constant play of rippling reflections, of light and shade set against a background of luxuriant plants or mysterious stones. Water can soothe and relax jangled nerves, nurturing the human psyche in ways beyond conventional understanding. It is also a key element in attaining good feng shui in a garden because water symbolizes prosperity and attracts *ch'i*, whose flowing, unimpeded passage is essential to creating a harmonious and happy environment.

In feng shui the location of the water is essential. Traditionally, the water feature should be positioned in front of the house, but since Western gardens tend to be more extensive at the back this is where water features are most often created, and this can be problematic. So if you place a water feature here the direction, according to Compass School Feng Shui, is vital to success. Use the Water Dragon formula, to calculate the right position. The best ponds have curved edges with large surface areas to provide a healthy habitat for wildlife.

style file

▲
A path can be allowed to wind through a garden and lead to a pleasant, sunny seating area, surrounded by shrubs and aromatic herbs.

◄
In this lovely country garden the stone path looks as though it has been there for years. The pretty pink and red flowers around it are very *yang*.

▼
A curvy, grass path can be created by designing the adjoining floral borders so that fast-growing shrubs sprawl over, or are cut back from the area.

▲
Different materials can work well together. Here, narrow paving slabs have been combined with pebbles.

Paths

Pleasurable, winding paths are at the heart of the feng shui garden. They are a vital ingredient for the easily controllable conduit of *ch'i*. However, all too often a garden path is a hotchpotch of leftover paving slabs, or hastily laid concrete. Yet, with some forethought and a modest budget, even the most unpromising eyesore can be transformed into a meandering walkway edged with delicate creeping plants.

Curved paths serve many purposes. They can create informal subdivisions within the space, lead naturally into circular paved areas, or form spiralling shapes snaking through the garden which create a flowing passageway for *ch'i*. Ideally, paths, patios, steps and walls should be made in the same materials. Appealing mixes for path designs include gray flagstones edged with red brick pavers and bricks laid in a winding herringbone pattern.

Edging plants – sprawling or spilling – help age pathways and also bring scent – try herbs such as prostrate rosemary or lavender – and color which can achieve balance between the Five Elements.

style file

◄
The warm glow of candles in a garden will help to bring in some *yang* energy. Special aromatic ones will also repel irritating mosquitoes.

▼
Hanging lanterns from trees or wall hooks in the South of your garden will enhance the Fire Element.

Lighting

Placing lights in your garden can create a warm, inviting glow and give it a more balanced, relaxed feel. They can enhance summer eating areas or be used to highlight seasonal planting, such as the spectacular reds and browns of autumn or the blue, pink, yellow and white blossoms of spring. Lights represent the Fire Element and give out positive *yang* energy, so can be used to create auspicious feng shui.

Using lanterns is especially potent in the South of any garden, as this area symbolizes Fire. When lights are small and non-threatening, they create good fortune in every part of the garden. Clever use of lighting is also an effective way of harnessing Earth luck and thereby enhancing and activating Family Relationship luck.

Using light to energize good areas of the garden and to repel problems can bring about major improvements to your garden feng shui. It can increase the potency of specific elemental forces and also attract both Recognition and Fame.

Eating out in the garden is one of the joys of summer. Lighting the area with lanterns, candles or flares adds romance and atmosphere, and also brings in positive energy.

▼ Garden lighting can be soft and subtle. Place lights in the shrubbery or behind rocks for a more ambient lighting effect.

▼ This glorious, rather Eastern looking light, will cast a glow of many colors in the garden.

style file

Planting

Plants are the core of every garden, but a feng shui garden requires further considerations. Combining plants with foliage that contrasts in both color and texture not only looks appealing, but will help balance *yin* and *yang*.

Small shrubs are best in the Southern area – the Phoenix hill – of the feng shui garden. They help form a seamless transition from the taller plantings, which should dominate the garden's Dragon 'quarter' (to the right of the front door, looking out), to the lower growing flowering plants in the area of the garden that is overseen by the Tiger (to the left of the front door).

Shrubs which can be useful for their positive influence in the feng shui garden include camellias and roses, but there are many others such as forsythia, shrubby clematis, and rhododendron.

In the East of the garden, which is governed by the Green Dragon, grow trees such as the Chinese dove tree (*Davidia involucrata*) and silk tree (*Albizia julibrissia* f. rosea) as well as their weeping forms. For fragrance, lilacs have a lot to offer: look for 'Mme Lemoine' (white, double flowers) or 'Souvenir de Louis Spaeth' (red). In the White Tiger or the Western area, grow flowers, especially scented varieties, and combine with low-growing shrubs.

◄
Orangey-red flowers make a strong impact in the garden. If you plant them in the South you will enhance your Recognition and Fame sectors.

▼
Poppies give a very unstructured feel to a large garden, and their strong red color is very *yang*.

▼
Tall-growing trees should be harmonized with low-growing shrubs and flowers in a feng shui garden.

▲
A garden needs to be a good mix of *yin* and *yang* energies. So experiment with combinations of different colored plants, evergreens, shapes and textures to achieve a comfortable balance.

▲

Painted trellis can
conceal unsightly
walls and fences

as well as be a
good support for
climbing plants.

▲

When eating out
in the summer,
adequate shade is
a necessity. This
colonial-style
umbrella is large
enough to shield
both table and
chairs.

▶

Terracotta pots
look good with
flowering plants or
herbs. They bring
warmth and good
Earth energies into
the garden. Place
them in the
Southwest to
enhance your
Marriage and
Romance sector.

► Umbrellas are essential for shade when eating or relaxing in a sunny garden.

▼ Ideally, place a metal bench in the West of your garden as it will boost the energies in this area.

Accessories

Once you have resolved the layout and the planting of your garden, you need to think about what accessories you can add to enhance it. Having barbecues and eating out is a popular summer pastime, so choosing the right furniture is important.

Rounded tables are best as they don't give off any cutting *ch'i*. Alternatively, choose a table with as few sharp edges as possible and cover it with a cloth when in use. Chairs with flowing curves will enhance the flow of *ch'i*. Decide on softwood (*yin*) or hardwood (*yang*) furniture depending on what else is in your environment Umbrellas in natural fabrics can be used to shield the excessive energy of the sun.

Big round earthenware pots, which symbolize the Earth element, can be a focus part of the garden. Place them to enhance the Southwest (Marriage and Romance) and the Northeast (Education and Knowledge) sectors.

Different types of trellis can be used to liven up dull fences or blank walls. Trailing plants or shrubs can be grown up them to add extra color or to conceal any sharp edges from which harmful cutting *ch'i* could emanate.

Picture Credits

Photographs:

IPC Associates: 1, 9, 37 (top right), 40 (all), 41 (all), 79 (bottom left), 88 (all), 89, 90, 92 (top), 93, 100 (all), 101, 102 (top), 103, 106 (all), 107 (bottom left), 110, 111, 112, 113 (all), 114 (all), 115 (all), 124 (all), 125 (all), 127, 140 (all), 141 (all), 142 (bottom), 144–145, 146 (middle), 148 (top), 150 (all), 151 (top and bottom right), 154 (top left and bottom), 155 (all)

Feng Shui for Modern Living **magazine:** 2, 3, 5 (all), 10, 11 (left and center), 17 (top right and bottom left), 18 (top), 20 (top and bottom right), 21 (both), 22, 24 (all), 25, 30 (bottom), 31 (top), 32 (top and middle), 33 (all), 34 (all), 35 (all), 39 (right), 58, 60 (all), 61 (all), 62 (all), 63 (all), 71 (left, middle and bottom), 73 (bottom), 75 (all), 82 (all), 83, 84, 94 (all), 95 (all), 97 (top and middle right), 98 (all), 98–99, 99 (all), 104 104–105, 105 (all), 118 (top), 119, 120 (bottom), 121 (bottom), 136 (all), 137, 138, 138–139, 139 (bottom), 152 (top)

Robert Harding Picture Library: 8, 11 (right and bottom), 12, 13 (all), 14 (top), 15, 16, 17 (top left and bottom right), 23, 30 (top), 32 (bottom), 36 (all), 37 (top left and right, bottom left), 38 (middle), 39 (top and bottom left), 43, 44–45,

46, 47, 48–49, 49, 50–51, 52, 53, 54 (all), 55, 56–57, 59, 64, 65, 66 (all), 67, 68, 69 (all), 73 (top and middle), 79 (top and bottom right), 81 (all), 85 (all), 86, 87 (top left and bottom), 91, 92 (bottom), 102 (bottom), 107 (bottom right), 108 (all), 109 (all), 126, 129, 132 (all), 133 (all), 134, 134–135, 135 (all)

Science and Society Picture Library: 14 (bottom)

The Holding Company: 18 (bottom left and right), 19, 20 (bottom left)

The Decorative Fabrics Gallery: 28, 29

Garden Picture Library: Garden Picture Library/Marie O'Hara: 31 (bottom), Garden Picture Library/ JS Sira: 38 (bottom), Garden Picture Library/Gary Rogers: 80, Garden Picture Library/Brigitte Thomas: 142 (left), Garden Picture Library/Juliette Wade: 143, Garden Picture Library/Ron Evans: 144, Garden Picture Library/Roger Hyam: 145, Garden Picture Library/Ron Sutherland: 146 (top right), Garden Picture Library/ Steven Wooster: 146 (bottom left), Garden Picture Library/Marie O'Hara: 146 (bottom right), Garden Picture Library/Steven

Wooster: 147 (top), Garden Picture Library/Ron Sutherland: 147 (bottom), Garden Picture Library/ Henk Dijkman: 148 (bottom), Garden Picture Library Ron Sutherland: 149 (top), Garden Picture Library/Howard Rice: 149 (bottom), Garden Picture Library/ Tim Griffith: 151 (bottom left), Garden Picture Library/Juliette Wade: 152 (bottom), Garden Picture Library/Howard Rice: 153 (left), Garden Picture Library/Eric Crichton: 153 (right), Garden Picture Library/Ron Sutherland: 154 (top right)

Monkwell: 70, 71 (right)

Shadwell: 72, 74

Crucial Trading: 87 (right)

Ligne Roset: 96–97 (top), 97 (bottom right), 107 (top)

Intermura: 96 (bottom)

Yellow Diva: 97 (bottom left)

McCord: 104 (middle)

Hansgrohe: 118 (bottom), 120 (top), 121

Elizabeth Whiting Associates: 128, 130 (top), 131 (top)

Acknowledgments

Artworks:

***Feng Shui for Modern Living* magazine:** 26, 27, 28, 61, 76, 77

Kate Simunek/Cima Books: 91, 102, 110, 120, 130, 139

The authors would like to acknowledge the contributions to this book from the following people:

Helen Oon, **Nikoletta Stamatatos**, **Lillian Too**, **Gina Lazenby**, **Nicola Stocken**, **Jonathan Edwards**, **Denise Linn**, **Master Yap Leong** and **Jon Sandifer**.

Mary Lambert is based in London and conducts feng shui consultations for small businesses and homes.

The authors would also like to thank the following companies whose help in providing images was invaluable:

Barnett Lawson Trimmings Ltd, **Crucial Trading**, **The Decorative Fabrics Gallery**, **The Holding Company**, **Intermura**, **Kartell**, **Ligne Roset**, **McCord**, **Monkwell**, **Shadwell** and **Yellow Diva**.

Index